the

NEW YORK

AGENT

BOOK

10th Edition

Tenth Edition 2016

©1987, 1990, 1993, 1995, 1998, 2001, 2004, 2007, 2016
ISBN 978-1-878355-24-9
ISSN 1058-1928

Other books by K Callan:

An Actor's Workbook
The Los Angeles Agent Book
How to Sell Yourself as an Actor
Directing Your Directing Career
The Script Is Finished, Now What Do I Do?
The Life of the Party

Illustration: Ohara Hale
Photography : Timothy Fielding
Editing: Nicholas Hormann
Art Direction: Tom Devine

Secure permission from
kcallan@swedenpress.com.
or
Sweden Press
P.O. Box 1612
Studio City, CA 91614

Table of Contents

chapter 1

Understanding the Actor's Life

Directors, producers, agents and civilians (people not in the business) frequently tell me that my industry books follow a circuitous route. Actors never say that. They know the business is a circuitous route. You enter the circle anyplace and don't get to choose where.

No matter where you enter, the ups and downs of the actor's life produce anxiety at almost every step. The periods of heat in a career make an actor think he will never be unemployed again no matter what he has witnessed or experienced before. The periods of unemployment produce the opposite reaction : "I'll never work again. It was all an accident. Now they know I can't act. I just fooled them before."

Some young actors waltz in, get attention, an agent and a job and aren't seriously unemployed for ten or twenty years. When things inevitably slow down, they have to learn the business skills that other less fortunate actors began to learn on day one. There are no steps to be skipped as it turns out. We all just take them at different times.

Although some actors never have to find a niche for themselves, most of us spend years figuring out just where we fit in. If you weigh five hundred pounds, it doesn't take a degree to figure out that you're going to play the fat one. If you go on a diet and become a more average size, casting directors will have a harder time pegging which one you are and so might you. This is not to say that if you are easily typecast your life is a bed of roses, but it can be a lot easier.

So, Self-Knowledge could be chapter one for one actor and the end of the book for another. An actor who already has an agent might feel justified in starting with Chapter Eleven because he wants to change agents while a newcomer in town might feel that divorce is not the problem. At this point, all he wants is an agent. Any agent.

In fact, a beginning actor would gain insight from that chapter. That information could alert him to potential warning signs when he is looking for his first agent, and Chapter Three might prompt the seasoned actor to reexamine all the things his agent does do for him.

This book deals with all aspects of actor/agent relationships at various stages of actors' careers: the first agent, the freelance alliance, the exclusive relationship, confronting the agent with problems, salvaging the bond, and if need be, leaving the partnership.

There is information for the newcomer, help for the seasoned actor and encouragement for all. My consciousness has been raised as a result of meeting and interviewing hundreds of agents in New York and Los Angeles. The process of interviewing them was just like every other part of the business, sometimes scary, sometimes wonderful and sometimes painful, but always a challenge.

Mostly the agents were charming, interesting, smart, dynamic and warm. This is why research is important. They all look great when they want to sign you, but you really can't tell a book by its cover.

Regardless of the circular nature of the business, my strong advice to you is to read straight through this book and not skip around. The first part provides background to critically understanding the information in the latter part of the book.

Fight the urge to run to the agency listings and read about this agent or that. Until you digest more criteria regarding evaluating agents you may find yourself just as confused as before.

If you read the agents' quotes with some perception, you will gain insights not only into their character but into how the business really runs. You will notice whose philosophy coincides with yours. Taken by themselves the quotes might only be interesting but considered in context and played against the insights of other agents, they are revealing and educational.

I have quoted a few agents who can't be on your wishlist either because they are now managers (Tim Angle, Gene Parseghian), out of the business (Joanna Ross, Lynn Moore Oliver), or deceased (Michael Kingman, Barry Douglas, Beverly Anderson, Fifi Oscard, Jerry Kahn, Shep Pamplin). Even though you won't be able to consider them as possible business partners, I feel their insights are particularly valuable. In the Index, they are listed as mentors.

Check all office addresses before sending snail mail and verify email addresses via IMDbPro. Every effort has been made to be accurate, but agents move and computers goof. Call or check websites to see if they prefer electronic or hard copy submissions. Don't waste your picture and resume if the agent only accepts electronically.

Because I am asking the questions for all of us, if I've missed something you deem important, write to me at kcallan@swedenpress.com or by snail mail at Sweden Press at the address on the back of the book and tell me and I'll try to deal with it in my next book. Be sure to write something in the reference line that identifies you as a reader; I dump a lot of junk mail.

Wrap Up
The Actor's Life
✓ circuitous
✓ chaotic
✓ anxious
✓ mercurial
✓ exciting/depressing
✓ everyone takes the same steps, just at different times

Research
✓ vital

This Book
✓ read in sequence
✓ the early chapters inform the latter
✓ the agent quotes are critical and will help you understand them and the business.

chapter _2

Forewarned

The good news is that there have never been more jobs for actors in the city than there are today. There are 30 television shows currently in production plus features, cable shows, broadcast and reality shows. There are 26 shows listed as Daytime, Late Night, News and Talk shows. Theatremania lists 95 comedy shows, 173 plays, 40 shows for family and kids and on and on. You can read all the latest production news at nyc.gov/html/film/html/for_fans/current_productions.shtml plus 12.

Aside from film and television, there are all the jobs you can create and perform in your apartment for youtube and other online venues.

The bad news is that there are far more eager souls looking for work than there are jobs, but the good news is that not all of them are going to be organized, motivated, trained, persistent, balanced and resilient. It's up to you to make sure you are.

Getting a paying job in some form of entertainment is a difficult job, but lots of us have done it and all of us have been fresh off the bus at one time or another facing The Big Apple trying to figure out the best way to take a bite.

Although getting an agent isn't going to necessarily solve all your problems, it's a good step. A reputable agent's submission continues to be the actor's best bet for a job once an actor is trained and has a resume and a reel.

This book is dedicated to teaching you how to represent yourself until that reputable agent is interested in the job and then educating you how to interview all those agents with the best criteria possible for getting the agent you need for the career you want.

As with any business, the way to survive and prosper is to see how you can manipulate the energy of the marketplace to your advantage. If you were a saddle maker when automobiles were invented, you could whine or you could figure out how to make seats for cars.

Oprah Winfrey studied to be an actress, switched to media and began a career as a broadcaster and still managed to be nominated for Oscars for *The Color Purple* and *Selma*.

You never know where your entrepreneurial talents will take you. The one thing we know is true, however, is that an investment of positive energy always pays off.

With that in mind, whether you're just starting in the business and trying to figure out your first step or whether you've been around a while and suddenly find yourself agent-free, take heart and a big breath.

Anything is possible.

Wrap Up

The Business

✓ lots of jobs available
✓ lots of eager actors
✓ need to be organized, motivated, trained, persistent, balanced and resilient
✓ sink or swim, it's your choice

chapter 3

Before You Leave Home

Three tools you need to bring with you to Manhattan are experience, education and enough money to support yourself for three years.

I would think most anyone who plans to assault the major marketplaces as an actor would have started acting in school plays and taken pretty much every chance to get up in front of people in their own home town. That includes any acting related ventures, whether it's singing *The Star Spangled Banner* at local baseball games, doing local television and radio commercials, producing podcasts, webisodes or short films or just generally being the center of any entertainment related ventures.

If you are still home and haven't been doing that, it's not too late. There is much to be learned in your local marketplace. If you're not far enough along to create your own projects, scour the newspaper and internet looking for productions filming locally looking for help. Even working as a gofer will yield a wealth of information and experience.

You might think these kinds of credits wouldn't count for much in Manhattan, but they were the beginning of your growth as an actor and entrepreneur and the mention on your resume shows your determination to learn all parts of the business and makes you a more attractive potential business partner to an agent. The more background you have before you assault one of the major marketplaces, the better, so if you are still in a position to get yourself trained, there are better and worse ways to go about it.

You Are Where You Study

I was a first generation college graduate and ignorant of all things college and lucky to get to go to any school. I didn't understand that not only could you get a better education at one school over another but that the contacts you would make could be life altering.

"I look at the school, and anyone who tells you they don't is lying to you," says producer Todd Black, who helped cast the Meryl Streep film "Hope Springs." *I'm gonna look much faster at a kid from a top school than from the University of Southern North Dakota.*

– The Hollywood Reporter[1]

If you are preparing to study, consider one of the important theatre schools if you can afford it and if they will accept you. It does make a difference. These schools are thought to be significantly superior to others and are universally accepted as the most comprehensive training for young actors. Their cachet instantly alerts the antennae of buyers (casting directors, agents, producers, directors, etc.). This is where the crème de la crème of new young actors – the next Meryl Streep and Bradley Cooper – are coming from (and did).

In 2014, *The Hollywood Reporter* put together a list of the top acting schools in the country supposedly based on research with members of The Casting Society of America. I'm respectful of the list and am printing the names of the schools here, but as I went to the website of each of these schools and did my own research, it was hard for me to understand how some schools got on that list.

For instance, the website of Depauw makes it difficult to even find acting and related classes. So, though I'm copying the *Hollywood Reporter's* list here below, I've edited it heavily. Some websites have little to say about the school other than that their students get to intern with big names in Los Angeles or were exposed to top agents and casting directors via a showcase upon graduation or had access to great guest speakers. You could say that about most schools on the list, and to access great speakers, you could just watch *Inside the Actors Studio.*

So, I've streamlined the list somewhat, eliminated some references and supplied my own. I invite you to look at the original list hollywoodreporter.com/news/top-25-drama-schools-world-558898 and to go to the website of any school that catches your eye and draw your own conclusions.

I found my website visits illuminating. For instance, I always thought of Cal Arts as a place for visual artists, but after reading its history and the continuing journey of the school, it now strikes as the best possible place for an all round arts education that would help you find your artistic focus in ways you might never have thought of. As in many elite theatre schools, your fellow students would be as inspiring as the staff.

This Top School list (edited here for format and clarity) first appeared in the June 7, 2014 issue of *The Hollywood Reporter Magazine*.

1. The Juilliard School, New York City: Juilliard won't mollycoddle you, but it may make you famous. 1981 alum Kevin Spacey told a student group that when he protested his tough treatment by a teacher who likened his voice to frayed rope: "She said, 'You're an idiot. Don't you realize that I'm the hardest on you because I think you're the most talented, but I also know you're the laziest?' And she was right." Graduates emerge with formidable language skills, script savvy and thick skins. Always a great launchpad, Juilliard just added a $10 million grant funding full tuition and stipends for top students. Notable alums: Jessica Chastain, Laura Linney, Viola Davis, Patti LuPone, Kelsey Grammar, Robin Williams, Adam Driver.

2. Yale School of Drama, New Haven: At Yale, students are center stage of the national theatre world, with a shot at movies and TV too. Since dean and artistic director James Bundy assumed leadership of the Yale Rep in 2002, he has produced more than 20 premieres of original dramatic works, including two Pulitzer finalists. Adds Bundy, "You will see, for instance, that 13 Tony Award nominees this year are graduates of the school and/or current members of the faculty." One Casting Society of America member said, "Their graduates feel like an elite corps of acting engineers: precise, well-read and eerily calm." Notable Alums: Meryl Streep, Patricia Clarkson, Liev Schreiber, Lupita Nyong'o, Paul Giamatti, Sigourney Weaver, Angela Bassett.

3. NYU, Tisch School of the Arts, New York City: Tisch's BFA program got high marks from the CSA (Casting Society of America), and its MFAs are even more esteemed. Says CSA member Monika Mikkelsen, "They have a power city to draw from, an acting school, directors, writers and filmmaking programs, and students are well-rounded and clear on the very hard course of life they have chosen for themselves." Felicity Huffman has said that if it weren't for NYU, she might not have had a career. Other notable alums: Alec Baldwin, Anna Kendrick and Jeremy Piven.

4. Carnegie Mellon University, Pittsburgh: Founded in 1914, ten years before Yale's drama school, CMU has produced winners of six Oscars, 24 Tonys and 95 Emmys, including two for Ted Danson, who said, "I really do owe everything to CMU. It set the tone for my life. I love the process, and I learned to love the process here." Other notable alums: Rob Marshall, Steven Bochco, Holly Hunter, Zachary Quinto.

5. London Academy of Music and Dramatic Arts, London: Open since 1861, LAMDA grads like *Imitation Game* star Benedict Cumberbatch routinely cross the pond. Other notable alums: Chris O'Dowd, John Lithgow, Jim Broadbent, Donald Sutherland.

6. Royal Academy of Dramatic Art, London: RADA doesn't dump its students on the job market. It assigns each grad at least two RADA "buddies" – pros with at least three years of experience, as mentors. Notable alums: Clive Owen, Diana Rigg, Tom Wilkinson.

7. University of North Carolina School of the Arts, Winston-Salem: UNCSA accepts about five percent of applicants. Alums got three 2012 Tony nominations. New drama dean Carl Forsman, a Drama Desk and Obie winner himself, plans graduate showcases in New York and LA. "Not a day goes by without our hearing about a drama alum who won a role in a film, on TV, at a regional theatre or on Broadway," says chancellor John Mauceri. Notable alums: Mary-Louise Parker, Jada Pinkett Smith, Chris Parnell, Tom Hulce, Terrence Mann.

8. National Institute of Dramatic Art, Kensington, Australia: Only four percent of applicants pass auditions and enter NIDA. "As things have gotten more international, I always make sure that I know about the graduating classes in Australia," says CSA member Margery Simkin, who cast *Pacific Rim*. Notable alums: Baz Luhrmann, Mel Gibson, Cate Blanchett, Hugo Weaving, Judy Davis.

9. Northwestern University, Evanston: Lionel Logue, whose unorthodox methods of therapy were dramatized in *The King's Speech,* was trained at Northwestern. The school's "Purple Mafia" includes the first female studio chief (Sherry Lansing), the first fictional female vice president (Julia Louis-Dreyfus), the second woman to win a directing Tony (Mary Zimmerman) and triple Oscar-nominated writer John Logan. A formal relationship with the Steppenwolf Theatre also adds cachet to this universally respected school. Notable alums: Stephen Colbert, Warren Beatty, Seth Myers, Pharrell Williams, Greg Berlanti.

10. Purchase College State University of New York, Purchase: The acting BFA program at SUNY Purchase is one of four in the nation that meets the standards of the Consortium of Conservatory Theatre Training Programs. They do not offer training in musical theatre. Graduates work consistently on and off Broadway, in films, on television and in other related media. Notable alums: Melissa Leo, Edie Falco, Stanley Tucci.

11. The Actor's Studio, Pace University, New York City: Method acting was invented at the Actors Studio where Brando, Pacino and De Niro got their start – not at this campus of The Actor's Studio, though the Pace program is the only MFA program sanctioned by the Actor's

Studio and does carry on the Stanislavski tradition. Notable alums: Chris Stack, Xanthe Elbrick, Bradley Cooper.

12. Guildhall School of Music & Drama, London: Third year actors at Guildhall spend their final year performing in public plays and musicals. Notable alums: Ewan McGregor, Eileen Atkins, Orlando Bloom, Michelle Dockery, Joseph Fiennes, George Martin.

13. American Conservatory Theater, San Francisco: A.C.T. has earned its own Tony and welcomed 7 million patrons. Its kids program produced Winona Ryder and Nicolas Cage. Notable alums: Annette Bening, Denzel Washington, Delroy Lindo, Elizabeth Banks.

14. UC San Diego, San Diego: Sharing shops and staff with the Tony-winning La Jolla Playhouse, UCSD puts on 15 productions a year. There are 200 undergrads and 60 MFAs culled from 500 applicants. Notable alums: Danny Burstein, James Avery.

15. California Institute of the Arts, Valencia: Founded and created by Walt Disney, CalArts was named America's top college for students in the arts by Newsweek in 2011. The focus is on the development of artistic talent. Their website is worth a visit: calarts.edu/about/history. Notable alums: Ed Harris, Tim Burton, John Lassiter, Don Cheadle.

16. Bristol Old Vic, Bristol, UK: The 250-year-old Old Vic is the UK's oldest continuously working theatre. The school, founded by Laurence Olivier in 1946, is mainly an undergraduate program but accepts up to 14 grad students a year. Notable alums: Daniel Day-Lewis, Jeremy Irons, Miranda Richardson, Patrick Stewart, Olivia Williams.

17. National Institute of Dramatic Art Kensington, Australia: Aided by the success of its long-admired undergraduate program, NIDA launched MFA programs for writing and directing in 2014.

Notable alums: Mel Gibson, Baz Luhrmann, Judy Davis, Cate Blanchett, Toni Collette, Colin Friels.

18. DePaul University, Chicago: The 6-to-1 student-teacher ratio at this Catholic university makes this small program one of the more intimate acting school experiences. Hard to tell from their website just what acting courses are offered. Notable alums: Stana Katic, Gillian Anderson, Judy Greer, Joe Mantegna, Elizabeth Perkins, John C. Reilly.

19. Columbia University, New York City: In addition to graduating three presidents (Barack Obama, Theodore Roosevelt, Franklin Roosevelt) and our first Secretary of the Treasury, Alexander Hamilton, what other credits are even worth mentioning? Notable alums: Brian Dennehy, Casey Affleck, Paul Robeson, Julia Stiles, Jake Gyllenhall, Kathryn Bigelow, Sofia Vergara, Maggie Gyllenhaal, Joan Rivers, Stanley Kubrick.

20. Boston University, Boston: BU's undergraduates at their College of Fine Arts get to create their own curriculum and are required to complete a professional internship in Boston, NYC or beyond. Study abroad is available the entire junior year to all Theatre Arts. Notable alums: Howard Stern, Julianne Moore, Rosie O'Donnell, Marisa Tomei.

21. Circle in the Square, New York City: "Circle," as it's known to students, is the only accredited training conservatory associated with a Broadway theatre. Notable alums: Felicity Huffman, Kevin Bacon, Idina Menzel, Benicio Del Toro and Lady Gaga.

22. University of Delaware, Newark: Many schools prune their students from semester to semester, but at UD, the class is taught to be a troupe. That philosophy, developed by artistic director, Sanford Robbins, gets results. Over the past 16 years, 94 percent of students seeking summer acting employment have managed to get it. Though

UD is no longer accepting students into their professional program, their website says full tuition waivers and full stipends are provided to all incoming students. Notable alum: Broadway director Susan Stroman.

23. The William Esper Studio, New York City: Esper worked for 17 years with Sanford Meisner – the guy who trained Gregory Peck, Diane Keaton, Eli Wallach, Maureen Stapleton, James Gandolfini, Jack Nicholson, Anthony Hopkins and Robert Duvall to name a tiny few. Notable alums: Kathy Bates, Richard Schiff, Larry David, Jeff Goldblum, Amy Schumer, Sam Rockwell, Timothy Olyphant.

24. University of Washington, Seattle: about 50 percent of students land gigs within 12 months of graduation. Notable alums: Rainn Wilson, Joel McHale, Jean Smart, Kyle MacLachlan.

Clearly, if you could go to one of these schools, your chances for success are enhanced, however not every student who studied at Yale is able to get work in the business and there are many very successful actors and stars who did not have the opportunity to train at these comprehensive, prestigious and expensive schools.

The leg up from these schools is mostly the immediate attention of agents and casting directors and the well rounded education in your craft, but once in the audition room, no one knows or cares where you went to school. It's all about your look and what you can do.

When researching schools, consider whether or not they offer a Bachelor of Fine Arts (BFA) or just a Bachelor of Arts (BA). The BFA degree appears to have more cachet. It's important to assess what your opportunities might be for actually getting onstage while at school. You really have to get onstage to learn and grow. Also check how recently the faculty has actually been working in the business.

The Hollywood Reporter list not withstanding, many agents concur that the two best musical theatre programs in the country belong to the Cincinnati Conservatory of Music and the Boston Conservatory of

Music. Each year, these schools' industry showcases attract almost every agent and casting director in New York City. Their graduates probably have the highest employment percentage of ANY drama school, musical or otherwise, graduate or undergraduate.

Even if you are educated at the best schools and arrive highly touted with interest from agents, retired WMA agent Joanna Ross told me there is still a period of adjustment:

When you come out of school, you gotta freak out for a while. Actors in high-powered training programs working night and day doing seven different things at once get out of school and suddenly there is no demand for their energy. It takes a year, at least, to learn to be unemployed. And they have to learn to deal with that. It happens to everybody. It's not just you.
— Joanna Ross

Although the connected schools may sometimes lead to auditions for immediate employment on a soap opera, in summer stock, in an off-Broadway play, more often it serves as a casting director's mental Rolodex of actors to use in future projects.
— New York Times[2]

Your first year out of one of those school, we can get you a lot of opportunities, it's up to you to prove yourself.
— Donald Birge, Stewart Talent

Even if you can't make it to a league school, all is not lost.

The truth is, a great performance in a connected school can jump-start a career, but if these kids have talent, they'll get noticed. They just won't be as fast out of the starting gate...they just have to do it the old-fashioned way by pounding the pavements, reading Back Stage, *calling up friends, going to see directors they know and knocking on agents' doors.*
— New York Times[3]

And maybe faster out of the gate isn't the best way to go anyway. Success in any business takes a toll on the persona. The more maturity you can gain first, the better your chance of weathering the shock of lots of money, instant friends and visibility. It's easier to deal with success when it comes gradually so you can adapt.

Too much too soon is too much too soon. No matter who you are, the career ebbs and flows. Stardom is just unemployment at a higher rate of pay.

And speaking of pay brings up the third important tool to bring with you to New York: money. You need an emergency fund and a conservative approach to your money or you could set your career back a few years just digging out.

A cautionary and educational tale about a young actor and his money can be found in the archives of my monthly column at *actorsink.com*. It's too long to print here, but if you can actually hear the message at this stage of your life, it could make a big difference to you across the board. Or you might just have to learn the hard way, but just in case, it's worth the effort to check out *The Actor and Money*. *nowcasting.com/actorsink/article.php?articleID=3428&lastupdate=1341622279*

Start listening to money guru Dave Ramsey daveramsey.com and check out his webpage. His philosophy would serve you well.

Wrap Up
Experience

✓ school plays

✓ local showbiz experience

✓ local civic events

✓ local radio and television commercials

✓ your own creations

Training

✓ connected schools helpful but can only do so much

✓ if you are trained and determined, everything evens out, it may just take longer

Money

✓ have emergency fund

✓ learn how to manage money

✓ Dave Ramsey

chapter 4

Welcome to the Big Apple

Now that you've exhausted all the opportunities at home, trained and created an emergency fund, you are finally ready to tackle Manhattan. As training for the impossible challenge of making a living as an actor, your first task will be to get acquainted with the city and get a place to live in New York.

Getting to Know the City

It's easy to get around the island of Manhattan. If you are directionally challenged, this is your chance to finally understand about north, south, east, and west. The Hudson River is west and guess where the East River is?

As you travel uptown (north), the numbers get larger and as you go downtown toward Wall Street, Chinatown, and the Statue of Liberty (south), the numbers get smaller. The numbers stop at Houston Street (pronounced "how-ston") and become Delancey, Spring, etc.

The next quickest way to get anywhere is on a bicycle, if you have the courage. That's too scary for me, so I walk. Cabs are expensive and frequently very slow. The fastest transportation is the subway which requires MetroCards. You can buy them at banks, some newsstands and in machines at most subway stations. Many stations don't have manned token booths at all times, so have appropriate bills or a credit card and don't expect directions.

There are subways that only go up and down the East Side (Lexington Avenue) and some that only go up and down the West Side (7th Avenue) and some (the E & F) that do both. There are some that only go crosstown (14th Street, 42nd Street and 59th Street). For more info: mta.info/nyct/subway/.

Most smart phones have awesome apps that tell you where the closest subway is and how to get where you are going. Download one first thing, but don't get dependent on them, you need to learn your way around.

Buses are great for shorter hops and accept Metrocards or exact change. Check mta.info/nyct/bus/howto_bus.htm/a/metrocards.htm.

I can walk across town in about twenty minutes; you probably can too. Crosstown blocks go east and west and are about three times as long as downtown blocks which go north and south. It takes about the same amount of time to walk from 42nd to 59th Streets as it takes to go from Lexington Avenue to Broadway.

In order to find the nearest cross street for your destination, check google.com/maps or ny.com/locator. For New York City transportation info try travel.howstuffworks.com/new-york-city-guide1.

Another way to get a handful of excellent Manhattan information is to pick up *The Official City Guide*, available at most hotels and/or online at cityguideny.com. I don't think I've seen a better source of maps and information about what's going on in Manhattan. It includes useful phone numbers and a reference page detailing cross streets relative to the address. Another useful link is newyorkcity.com.

Get a Place to Live
Even though it's New York, the problem is not unsolvable. The Drama Book Shop (250 West 40th Street), most acting schools and the acting unions all have bulletin boards listing sublets that might give you temporary housing while you get your bearings. Other good housing resources are craigslist.com and airbnb.com.

There is actor-friendly housing in West Beth (downtown in the West Village) and The Manhattan Plaza (midtown on the West Side). Both are artistic communities with subsidized housing and long waiting lists, but since actors are frequently out of town for jobs, sublets are available. Both of these artists' havens offer classes and are plugged into the creative forces of the city.

Areas in which rents might be cheaper are the Lower East Side, below Wall Street, Chinatown, Harlem, the Upper West Side and some areas of what used to be called Hell's Kitchen in the far West 40s. All the cool people are moving to Brooklyn or Long Island City the first stop past Grand Central on the #7 train in Queens. Not that far away and cheaper.

The Visitor's Bureau (nycgo.com) has data on Youth Hostels. And for city housing help, nyc.gov/html/housinginfo/html/home/home.shtml.

There are those fabled $400 per month apartments that keep us all salivating but they have been occupied for hundreds of years by the same tenant and all their offspring. Don't stop yourself from finding suitable housing because you are waiting for one of those mythical deals. You don't want to use up all your good luck getting a swell apartment for 35¢. Save your luck for your big break and you'll be able to afford to pay full price.

More people are finding housing in Brooklyn, Queens, New Jersey and Staten Island. When I arrived in New York, I briefly considered New Jersey since I had children, but after much soul-searching, I realized that my dream was to come to New York City. I decided that if I was going to starve, it would be while living my dream all the way. Not everyone's dream is so particularized. These days, it's very cool to live out of Manhattan.

The next thing you need to do is to get a job, and not just for financial survival.

A Job Gives Form to Your Life

Having a job gives form to your life, a place to go every day, a family of people to relate to and helps you feel as though you are part of the city and not just a tourist.

Nothing feeds depression more than sitting at home alone in a strange city. Even if you know your way around, you'll find that as time goes on, activity is the friend of the actor. Depression feeds on itself and must not be allowed to get out of hand.

Don't drain your emergency fund. If you allow yourself to be broke you'll just drag yourself down. This is something you can control. Being a starving actor doesn't work. What works is to take care of yourself so that you are healthy and have money in your pocket and not eternally worried about paying your bills. Don't keep taking money from your parents, be responsible for yourself and get a job.

Before an actor begins to look for an agent, he should establish a secure foundation. He or she needs a place to live and/ or a job, some friends to talk to, and pictures or at least a facsimile of pictures. It's very important that they have a comfortable place to go to during the day and be settled so they don't carry any more anxiety than necessary into an agent or manager's office.

Some actors think an agent or a manager will turn into a surrogate mother-father-teacher-confessor. That isn't his role. Actors get disappointed when they aren't taken care of right away. I think it's better to come in as a fully secure person so you can be sold that way. Otherwise, too much development time is wasted.
– Gary Krasny, The Krasny Office

If you can combine a showbiz job with flexible hours permitting auditions, that's the best of all possibilities. Always be available. Don't say you are an actor if you have a 9-to-5 job. If you must waitress, do it at night.
– Sharon Carry, Carry Company

Casting Society of America Job File

Sitting in an agent's office waiting for an appointment, I met a young actor who was manning the phones. He told me he has worked as a casting assistant in both Los Angeles and New York and had come to his present job by faxing his resume to the Casting Society of America (castingsociety.com) job file.

The pay is small, but he said the access to the business was well worth it. He said he wouldn't trade a higher salary for the business maturity he had acquired.

As soon as you are working in the business in any category, you are in the system and on your way. I don't want to imply that coming up with one of these jobs is the easiest task in the world, but it is definitely worth the effort.

Before your resume is ready for you to be interviewing agents as possible business partners, you may find yourself encountering them either in your work or on a social level. Just as doctors don't like to listen to your symptoms at a party, an agent wants to party in peace. Be a professional and talk about something other than your career. Agents prefer to do business in their offices. Don't introduce yourself as an actor unless you are asked what you do. If you detect signs of interest from anyone, directors, producers, etc., follow up on it. Ask if there is anything you can do to help with a current project.

I know you are itching to look for an agent and become a working actor, but first things first; get situated, meet some people, store some good feelings and financial bank accounts. You will need them all.

Wrap Up
Geographical Resources
- ✓ maps
- ✓ NYC Convention Bureau
- ✓ Internet
- ✓ Google Maps
- ✓ smart phone apps

Finding a Place to Live
- ✓ Drama Book Shop bulletin boards
- ✓ union bulletin boards
- ✓ craigslist.com, airbnb.com

Your Day Job
- ✓ gives form to your life
- ✓ a family
- ✓ a place to go every day
- ✓ any showbiz job teaches you about the business

chapter _5

Avenues of Opportunity

Many actors regularly curse and malign them, either feeling rejected that they can't get an agent to talk to them, or frustrated once they have an agent simply because of their unrealistic expectations.

You can save yourself a lot of heartache and ultimately move your career along faster, if you take the time and effort to learn how the business really works, how agents do their jobs, and how the agent is not the only person who can make things happen for you.

Let's start by defining what an agent is and is not and what he does. Do you even need one at this point? Where would you find one? How can you get one to even meet with you and once there, what would you say? Are there rules of behavior? How can you tell if someone is a good agent? When is the right time to look for one? If they all want to sign you, how would you choose the right one? If no one wants to sign you, what will you tell your mother?

Unless your mother is an actress, she is never going to understand, so don't try. Those who have never pursued a job in show business (civilians and would-be actors who are still in school) can never understand what an actor goes through in pursuit of employment and/or an agent. So don't waste time on that conversation.

Just say: "Mom, I'm doing great. I'm unemployed right now and I don't have an agent, but that's part of the process. There are things I need to accomplish before it's time for me to look for an agent."

She's still not going to understand that, but it will mean something to her that you have a plan and it's something to say to her friends.

What Is An Agent?
To be a franchised agent, the agent must have a license to operate from the state, abide by SAG-AFTRA Agency Rules and Regulations, have some experience as an agent and put up a financial bond. None of this

guarantees the agent to be ethical, knowledgeable or effective. You'll have to check for yourself. For SAG-AFTRA franchise intel: *sagaftra.org/files/sag/documents/l-sag_franchise_application_in_la_for_ca_agents.pdf.*

Whether your agent fantasy includes the old-fashioned stereotype of cigar-chomping hustlers or the newer version of the cool customer decked out in Armani, many actors fantasize that the right agent holds the secret of success. Joanna Ross was an agent at William Morris before moving to Italy, but I'm still quoting her because her perspective on the actor/agent relationship is so insightful.

Actors feel that if they make the right choice, the agent is somehow going to make them a star and help them be successful or they're going to make the wrong choice and that's it. And that's just not it. No agent can make anybody a star or make him a better actor than he is. Agents are only avenues of opportunity.

That being the case, what do these Avenues of Opportunity do? The dictionary has several definitions for the word agent. By combining a couple, I've come up with one that works for show business: A force acting in place of another, effecting a certain result by driving, inciting, or setting in motion.

In its simplest incarnation, the agent, acting on your behalf, sets in motion a series of events that result in your having a shot at a job. He gets you meetings, interviews, and auditions. And he prays that you will get the job or at the very least make him look good by being brilliant at your audition.

When an actor grouses that the agent is not getting him out, he seems to think the agent doesn't want him to work, completely forgetting that if the actor doesn't work, the agent can't pay his rent. The actor also often overlooks the fact that his part of the partnership is to get the job.

It should be simple. After all, you've spent years perfecting your instrument, learning your craft, training your voice, strengthening your body, defining your personality, and building a resume that denotes credibility. Haven't you?

An Agent Prepares

While you have been working on every aspect of your craft, the agent has spent his time getting to know the business. He's seen every play, television show, and film. He's watched actors, writers, directors, and producers birth their careers and grow. He's tracked people at every level of the business. He has networked, stayed visible, and communicated. He's made it his business to meet and develop relationships with casting directors.

The agent *you want* only represents those actors whose work he personally knows. When he tells a casting director that an actor is perfect for the role and has the background for it, the casting director trusts his word. That's the way the agent builds credibility and it doesn't happen any faster than the building of the actor's resume.

In addition to getting the actor the right audition, the agent has to be prepared to negotiate a brilliant contract when the actor wins the job. That entails knowing all the rules and regulations of SAG-AFTRA and Actors' Equity, understanding the marketplace and knowing what others at similar career levels are getting for similar jobs.

He must have the courage, style and judgment to stand up to the buyers and must ask for appropriate money and billing for the actor without becoming grandiose and turning everyone off. The agent must also fight the temptation to sell the actor down the river in order to seal his own future relationships with the producer or casting director.

What Do Agents Think Their Job Is?

The Association of Talent Agents (ATA) is the official trade organization of talent agents. Their webpage provides a description of their role in an artist's life (agentassociation.com/frontdoor/faq.cfm88):

Creating opportunities for their clients is at the heart of what ATA agents do. Licensed and regulated by state and local government agencies, ATA agents are at the focal point of change in the industry and at the forefront of the development of new relationships for their clients. In an era of media consolidation and vertical integration in the industry, ATA agents are the artists' strongest allies.

In contrast to many other industry professionals, ATA agents are licensed and strictly regulated by state and local government agencies in California, New York and the other parts of the country where agents do business. In California, for example, ATA agents are not only licensed by the State Labor Commissioner and subject to annual review, but the artists' contracts are approved by the State Labor Commissioner. ATA agencies also work under negotiated agreements with DGA, WGA, AFTRA, Actors' Equity and AFM. While the SAG agreement expired in 2002, ATA agencies continue to work with actors under ATA state-approved agency contracts.

Agent Shep Pamplin has left the business now and we are poorer for it. He was wise:

Sometimes actors don't really consider all the work an agent may do for them that doesn't result in an appointment. The agent may have said your name many times to the casting director until the CD has heard it often enough that he begins to think you are actually working.

At that point, the actor happens to call the casting director himself and ends up with an appointment and subsequently a job. Now he calls his agent and says, "Well, hey. I got the job myself. Why should I pay you commission?" In my head, I'm going, "who sat down with you and told you how to dress? Who helped you select the photos you are using right now that got you that audition? Who helped you texture your resume? Who introduced you to the casting director? What makes you think you did that on your own?"

They don't see it. They don't see that, like a manager, I have taken them from here to there. I set up the auditions. Most actors don't realize the initial investment we make, the time, the energy, the phone calls, the mail, the hours of preparing the actor and getting them to the right places. There is no compensation for that until maybe two years down the road.

At that point, you've made them so good that someone else signs them anyway. There's not a lot of loyalty among actors. They'll always want the person who gets them the next job. They don't comprehend what we go through to get them ready for

that point where they can get a job.
— H. Shep Pamplin

It is unusual that an actor arrives on the scene poised enough to handle himself in the audition room. That kind of poise usually cannot be acquired without going through the struggle time. An agent who invests his time and energy in the struggle time should be rewarded, not discarded.

If you sign someone, if you agree to be their agent, no matter how big the agency gets, you've agreed to be there for them and that's your responsibility. I feel that I'm responsible for my clients' attitudes and for their self-confidence.
— Kenneth Kaplan, The Gersh Agency, Inc.

A young actor told me that while helping out in his agent's office he was able to look at his own records and see that he had been submitted over 1000 times before he got an actual audition. I wonder how many agents have been through that.

I offer hard work and honesty and demand the same in return. If I'm breaking my ass to get you an audition, you better show up.
— Martin Gage, BRS/Gage Talent Agency

Remember that your agent didn't sign on to be your therapist. One of the best agents I ever had wasn't willing to be my therapist. He did, however, initiate new business for me, was respected in the community, negotiated well, showed impeccable taste, and had access to everyone.

He also believed in me and retained that faith when I didn't win every audition. He gave me good notes on my performances, clued me in to mistakes I was making, and made a point of viewing my work at every opportunity and he returned my phone calls. That last item is a deal breaker as far as I am concerned.

A friend toiled for many years on a well-regarded series. She was happy to be working, but she was underpaid. She changed agents and doubled her salary. A year later she changed agents again: "They were good negotiators, but I couldn't stand talking to them."

You can't have everything.

Being a tough negotiator sometimes displaces graciousness. Your agent's job description isn't to be your friend, he's your business partner. You have to decide what you want and what you need.

Lynn Moore Oliver was still a Los Angeles agent when she offered a comprehensive picture of what agents are doing on our behalf, even when we can't tell they are even thinking about us.

I'm working on the belief that symbiotically we're going to build a career. While the actor isn't working, I'm paying for the phone, the stationery, the envelopes, the Breakdown Services (which is expensive), the rent, the overhead, stamps, all the things that one takes for granted in the normal turn of business.

All this is coming out of my pocket working as an employment agent, because that is really what I am. The actor is making no investment in my promoting his career. If the career is promoted, we both benefit and I take my 10% commission. Meanwhile, the overhead goes on for months, sometimes years with no income. The first thing the actor is going to say is, nothing's happening. My agent is not doing a good job. *What they forget is that I have actually invested money in their career and I've probably invested more money in the actor's career than he has, on an annual basis.*

– Lynn Moore Oliver

If you think about Lynn's words, you will understand why credible agents choose clients carefully. Looking at your actor friends, are there any that you would be willing to put on your list and pay to promote?

Puts things in perspective, doesn't it?

Wrap Up

Agent
- ✓ a force acting in place of another, effecting a certain result by driving, inciting, or setting in motion
- ✓ licensed by the state and franchised by SAG-AFTRA

Agent's Job
- ✓ to get the actor meetings, interviews, auditions, and to negotiate salary and billing

chapter 6

Your First Agent: You

There's good news and bad news. First the bad news: you're probably going to have to be your own first agent. Now the good news: nobody cares more about your career than you do, so your first agent is going to be incredibly motivated.

In order to attract an agent, you have to have something to sell. No matter how talented you are, if you don't have some way to show what you've got, you're all talk. Working up a scene for the agent's office will work for a few agents, but it's not enough.

Your focus should be to amass credits by appearing onstage and in student and independent films so an agent can find you – and so you can put together a professional audition DVD/electronic sample of your work.

This book is focused on actors who are already entrepreneurial. For those who need help in that department, get my marketing book, *How to Sell Yourself as an Actor*.

I know what you are thinking: "Swell. How am I going to amass credits and put together a professional sample without an agent? How am I ever going to get any work? How will I get smarter?"

By growing. Pick up *Back Stage* for casting notices or read it online, backstage.com. Check out the casting tab at Actors' Equity's website, actorsequity.org. You don't have to be a member for access. Become part of the actor's grapevine by joining a theatre group or getting into an acting class. Invite a group of actors to your place once a week to read a play aloud. Once you start expending energy in a smart way, things begin to happen. Sending out pictures and resumes is not a growth experience.

Grab a Back Stage *and start auditioning for everything! Then find a well-known and respected acting teacher who works with accomplished students. These two small*

actions will be the beginning of your show business networking. Teachers, friends and colleagues provide a conduit to your future agent or to a casting director.
— Jeanne Nicolosi, Nicolosi & Co., Inc.

I asked dance agent Thomas Scott the first thing dancers should do.

Start to study and become familiar with the choreographers. Begin to form relationships with working choreographers. Both Broadway Dance Center and Steps are dance studios where great working choreographers teach.
— Thomas Scott, DDO Artists Agency

Decide what you want to do. Narrow your focus. Do you want to sing? Dance? Be in movies? Be specific, get good headshots, and we'll plan it out and do it together.
— Lisa Price, The Price Group Talent

They are meeting us for the first time, we shouldn't meet them unless they do something better than a whole lot of other people. This is a town of specialities. Versatility is for grad school, but when you compete as an actor in New York, it's about being special not how many things you do.
— Jed Abrahams, Kazarian, Measures, Ruskin & Associates

Gain technique and skill. Nurture your look. You are your own product. Fine tuning your look is the most important thing.
— Thomas Scott, DDO Artists Agency

Contact everyone you know. Get to class. Get good headshots. If you are "soap" material, send your picture/resume to all the daytime casting directors.
— Diana Doussant, Leading Artists, Inc.

You can't have just one headshot anymore. Or have pictures taken by your friend with an amateur camera. Your headshot is your first selling point. Nobody said that being an artist is easy and an inexpensive profession. Musicians have to invest in their instruments, so do painters, sculptors etc. If you are an actor with big

aspirations you will invest in yourself as much as you can. Your mind (workshops, seminars), your body (gym), and other tools such as headshots, reels.
– Marius Bargielski, Metropolis Artists Agency

It's always been hard for someone right out of school. They don't know how tall the mountain is and how far they have to go, it's probably just the same as it usually is when anybody gets to town, they have to adjust to the city, they have to learn to support themselves, they have to learn to adjust to the audition.
– Renee Glicker, About Artists Agency

There are many different ways for actors to introduce themselves to the industry even when unrepresented. Whether it's a show you have mounted or something you put up on youtube, the important thing to remember is that anything you put out there should be looked upon as an audition for the most important person in the industry.
– Jed Abrahams, Kazarian, Measures, Ruskin & Associates

You're not going to just waltz in and meet agents and casting executives, but as you begin to make friends with others on your level in the business, you will be surprised how one thing leads to another.

The Actor's Job: Looking for Work

Becoming an actor is not an overnight process. A large part of being an actor on any level is looking for work. Don't equate being paid with being an actor.

You are already an actor. Even if you are a student actor, you're still an actor and you already have your first job: get a resume with decent credits onstage, on film and television. This will begin to season you as an actor, and if it's on camera, you will be building an electronic sample of your work.

What denotes decent credits?

Expectations for a young actor are different than for an older actor. The white space is your friend, it means you are fresh. Don't fib a lot of experience and try to act

older, you need training but your youth and meager resume is what you have to sell.
– Jed Abrahams, Kazarian, Measures, Ruskin & Associates

That said, your blank resume is probably not going to get you into any offices for them to see how young and fresh you are and though there have been a few young and particularly gorgeous or extremely wacky character people who got called in from blanketing the town with their pictures and blank resumes, that's a rarity.

In lieu of gorgeousness, wackiness or a diploma from one of the connected schools, take a breath and embrace your fate. You must build your resume and your relationships within the business, i.e., people you work with not those you meet at parties.

If you are able to score a good part in a decent venue that gets reviewed, an agent might see you and/or read your great reviews and agree to take a meeting with you.

If you hope to be cast in film and television you need to be able to deliver an example of your work. It should be no longer than five minutes (shorter is best) and show either one performance or a selection of scenes of your work. It's very difficult for an agent to get a casting director to meet you unless there is an electronic sample of your work, so focus on getting a DVD in your bag and an electronic sample online. Do every independent or student film you can. Commit to putting something online weekly. Grow.

Agents and casting executives view work endlessly and can tell quickly if you are of interest to them, so even if you have some great stuff, err on the side of brevity. It is better to have just one good scene from an actual job than many short moments of work or a scene produced just for the reel. Some agents will watch self-produced work and some will not. Most casting directors tell me that if they have time, they usually watch whatever is sent.

Technology and editors have gotten so skillful that it's easy to come up with a slick package if you have the money, but caution: slickness is no substitute for quality work. Casting directors can tell when it's all just tap dancing.

If you can't produce footage that shows you clearly in contemporary material playing a part that you could logically be cast for, then you aren't far enough along to show yourself. Better to wait. Patience.

What Agents Want in a Picture

The number one dictate about pictures is: What You See Is What You Get. Agents don't like surprises. If your picture looks like Jennifer Lopez and you look like Joan Cusack, the agent not going to be happy when he calls you in to read and you will be disappointed.

Your picture and your DVD are your main selling tools, so choose carefully. Pictures can be printed with or without a border. Some agents prefer a picture without, but borderless frequently costs more. Your name should be printed on the front, either superimposed over the photo or in the white space below. Name and contact information should be featured prominently on the resume.

Although the majority of actors hand out a closeup, more and more are using a 3/4 color shot. That's the industry standard for dancers. That said, many casting directors are getting your info online from your agent and a nice fat closeup is more impactful than a body shot unless you are a dancer.

The picture of you on your mother's piano is not necessarily the best for your selling tool. Be conscious of the jobs you are sent for when you choose your 8x10.

There are many good photographers in town whose business is taking actor headshots. They vary in price and product. I've gathered a list of favorites from agents, actors, and casting directors. Don't just choose one off the list. You need to do your own research.

The Internet has made shopping for a photographer easier. You can look at a number of pictures and evaluate why one picture appeals to you more than another. An expensive price tag doesn't guarantee a better picture. It's possible to get the perfect picture for under $200 and a picture you will never use at $900.

The consensus from agents seems to be that you should expect to pay $500-$600 for pictures. Photographers encourage hair and makeup, but that's more for them than you. It makes their job easier. Decide for yourself what you want. It's nice to be professionally put together, but make sure you can duplicate the look when you audition.

It takes time to meet personally with several photographers but it's worth the effort. It's not just that you need to meet the photographer, he needs to meet you and get a sense of who you are. My friend Mary's pictures were taken by a respected Los Angeles photographer and though technically perfect, they had a moodiness to them that had nothing to do with Mary's natural affability. The pictures were interesting but did not represent who Mary is and how she is cast.

If you choose the right photographer, you can get appropriate pictures and it can be fun.

When you schedule your headshot session, you are choosing to make a positive change in your career. It's something you should enjoy doing, and look forward to. Prepare for your shoot by treating yourself well, getting plenty of sleep, caring for your body, and allowing plenty of time to prepare. If you're nervous, bring a friend, and bring music that you like.
– Nick Coleman, photographer

Some actors I know have pictures taken by family members with digital cameras. With Photoshop at your fingertips, you can take out unwanted shadows and produce a pretty good picture on your own, however if you have the money to hire the right professional, it's worth it. Pictures are your agent's selling tools. Give them something that represents you.

And from personal experience, I would urge you not to get carried away with the beautiful/handsome picture unless you are Brad or Angelina. I had some great pictures taken and was totally in love with them. However, when I was able to step back and evaluate, I realized that those pictures, though flattering, were worthless to me. I am pretty, but I'm never going to be cast as "the pretty one", so there is no use in my trying to sell myself that way. One must be realistic. I take absolute responsibility for that gaffe. That photographer didn't really know my work. I had chosen him because his lighting, hair and makeup result in glamorous photos and I was having a vanity attack.

And how do you evaluate the effectiveness of your picture?

If you are getting a lot of auditions, but aren't booking work, the problem is not your headshot. If you are having trouble getting an agent to open your mail, or getting called into audition for casting directors, the problem could very well be your headshot. Is it high quality? Does it represent you well? Is it recent enough?
– Nick Coleman, photographer

Photographers

Richard Blinkoff (richardblinkoff.com) shoots, edits, proofs, retouches and prints his digital photos in his daylight studio in Chelsea. He also does any typesetting and graphic work you need to make other headshots, postcards or composite cards. He shoots from 36th Street on the West Side. 212-620-7883.

Tess Steinkolk (tsteinkolk.com) sounds great. She graduated from the American University in Washington D.C., a city in which she had an illustrious career not only at the White House during the Carter Administration, but also at the Smithsonian where she studied and was on staff. During that time she was house photographer for the Arena Stage. She moved to New York in 1981 and continues her amazing work.

The FAQ link on Tess' webpage answers every question from how much, to how many, to what to wear and on and on. Check it out and also look at her awesome pictures. 212-706-7062.

Dave Cross (davecrossphotography.com) has been a professional photographer in New York for over twenty years. After pursuing a career as an actor he decided to photograph actors instead of being one. In addition to shooting Broadway, soaps, movie performers and theatre companies, Cross' work has been seen in *The New York Times*, *Time-Out New York* and *Dance Magazine*. 212-279-6691.

Nick Coleman (colemanphotographix.com)is still working successfully as an actor/writer/director in film, television, theatre and independent film, but he still found time to carve out a successful career as a photographer. His graphic designs and artwork can be seen on book covers, theatrical posters, television ads, and as web graphics on internet sites and email blasts.

His webpage lays out all the fees and is a wealth of information beyond that. I particularly like his actors' jumpstart link. I think it's his actor-director-writer background that gives him the consciousness to ask all the right questions. 917-447-8057.

Actress/model/photographer **Jinsey Dauk** (jinsey.com) has been shooting pictures since the 8th grade. She studied and then taught photography at Wake Forest University in Winston-Salem, North Carolina. Since she also studied film production and psychiatry, she brings special sensitivities to her work. Her webpage is worth a look. There's a discount for checking out her work online instead of in her apartment/studio, so although that goes against my advice to meet the photographer first, it's worth $200 off the price. Her webpage intel will inform your choices no matter which photographer you eventually choose. I had trouble with her link so just googled Jinsey Dauk; you might have to do the same. 212-243-0652.

Glen Jussen Studio (jussenstudio.com) is high on agents' lists of photographers for kids and young adults. Kids under 16 (without a makeup artist) get a discounted rate of $300 for 50 images and one retouched image on a CD. 212-268-1340.

SAG-AFTRA forbids agents to suggest teachers, photographers, etc. because the union wants to avoid kickbacks at the expense of the actor, but some larger agencies have negotiated group discounts for their clients for webspace, pictures and classes. Because of SAG-AFTRA's concerns, if you ask an agent for a recommendation for classes and photographers, they frequently hand you a list.

Resume

A resume should be attached to the back of your 8x10 glossy or matte print so that as you turn the picture over front to back, the resume is right side up. The buyers see hundreds of resumes every day, so make yours simple and easy to read. No weird fonts.

If you have the luxury of a long resume, pick and choose what to list. When prospective employers see too much writing, their eyes glaze over and they won't read anything, so be brief.

There is an example on the next page to use as a guide. Lead with your strongest credits. If you have done more commercials than anything else, list that as your first category; if you are a singer, list music. You may live in a market where theatre credits are taken very seriously. If so, even though you may have done more commercials, lead with theatre. If all you have done is college theatre, list that. This is more than someone else has done and it will give the buyer an idea of parts you can play. Note that you were master of ceremonies for your town's Pioneer Day Celebration. If you sang at The Lion's Club program, list that.

Accomplishments that might seem trivial to you could be important to someone else, particularly if you phrase it right. If you are truly beginning and have nothing on your resume, list your training and a physical description along with the names of your teachers. Younger actors aren't expected to have credits.

The most important thing on your resume is your name and your agent's phone number. If you don't have an agent, get voice mail for work calls. It's more professional and it's safer. Don't use your personal phone number.

How to Structure Your Resume

I know you are proud of it, but it's not necessary to list union affiliation on your resume. The names of directors you have worked with are important to note. If you were in a production of *A Streetcar Named Desire* and you played Blanche, by all means say so. If you were

John Smith/Smith Agency 214-555-4489
6'2" 200 lbs, blonde hair, blue eyes

Theatre
Hamilton. . . . . directed by Thomas Kall
Fun Home. . . . . directed by Sam Gold

Film
Steve Jobs. . . . . directed by Danny Boyle
Man on a Ledge. . . . . directed by Asger Leth
The Book of Henry. . . . . directed by Colin Trevorrow

Television
The Affair. . . . . directed by Jeffrey Reiner
Madame Secretary. . . . . directed by Eric Stoltz
The Good Wife. . . . . directed by Rod Holcolb

Training
Acting. . . . . Karen Ludwig, William Esper, Sam Schacht
Singing. . . . . Andrea Green, Maryann Chalis
Dance. . . . . Andy Blankenbuehler, Christopher Gattelli

Special Skills
guitar, horseback riding, martial arts, street performer, Irish, Spanish,
British, Cockney, & French dialect, broadsword, fencing, certified yoga
instructor, circus skills, etc.

a neighbor, say that.

The casting director or agent wants to know how green you are; if
you have "carried" a show, that's important. Misrepresenting your work
is self-destructive. Not only can people check your credits online these
days, but you risk running into the casting director for that show who
will tell you that she doesn't recall casting you. Even worse, if you list
large roles that you have never played, you may not be able to measure

up to your reputation. Carrying a show is a much bigger deal than just having a nice part.

Open Calls

Although Equity Open Calls are limited to members of Equity, in 1988 the National Labor Relations Board required that producers hold open calls for non-union actors. These auditions can be harrowing, with hundreds of actors signing up to audition for a small number of jobs.

I represent a woman who was interested in being in Les Miz. *She felt strongly that she wanted to play Cossette and although I have a twenty year relationship with the casting directors, they were disinclined to bring her in. I encouraged her to go to the open call, she did, and she got the job.*
– Jim Wilhelm, DGRW

Actors' Equity surveyed 500 members and found that 47% had found jobs through open casting calls. In calls for chorus work, which has its own system, casting directors size up the hopefuls who show up and point to those who resemble the type they are seeking before holding auditions.
– The New York Times[4]

Although some do get jobs in musicals through open calls, all concerned say it's an endurance contest.

It's not just wearing for the actors; the producers, directors, and casting executives also find it daunting. And only a hundred were given a chance to sing half a song and hoof a few steps. Vincent G. Liff, the casting director for Big *and* Phantom of the Opera, *who turned away no less than 250 women for* Big *alone, called the turnout frightening but said the system, while patience-trying, was valuable. "We have cast dozens and dozens of people through these calls," Mr. Liff said.*
– The New York Times[5]

The most successful people in any business are smart, organized, and entrepreneurial, but almost no one starts out that way. It's like learning to walk: it takes a while before you can get your balance.

As you continue reading agents' remarks about what successful actors do, you will begin to develop an overview of the business that will help you in the process of representing yourself. It's essential to stay focused and specific, and to give up the natural urge to panic.

Bring the same creative problem-solving you use in preparing a scene to the business side of your career. You will not only be successful, you will begin to be more in control of your own destiny.

You're Only New Once

First impressions are indelible. That first day of school thing follows you for the rest of your life. How you behave on the first day of school is how your teachers will always think of you. No matter how great you are the second day, if you trip the first day, you're stuck with that. On the other hand, if you are a good guy that first day, you can trip many days thereafter and still get by on that good boy image.

If you have a meeting with a casting director and/or agent and aren't prepared, it's going to be hard to get another audition/meeting. My young friend "John" recently tripped. After being in town three years studying at a local conservatory, he met an industry professional who began acting as a mentor, answering questions and giving guidance. After John acquired a manager and was cast in an independent film that was going to pay for him to join SAG, the Industry Professional offered to get John a meeting with an agent.

Though the movie kept getting pushed for weather reasons, the fact that John had booked it convinced the IP who had still never seen John work that John was "far enough along" to be introduced to an agent even though he had never seen John's work.

This turned out to be a big mistake. John hadn't expected to be asked to perform and instead of saying that and asking to come back, he moved forward with a monologue and choked. The moment John left the office, the agent called the IP to ask why he had recommended such a green actor.

It turned out that John was not only green, but clueless. He had no idea that he had bombed and was missing any kind of antennae to measure how he had done. Acting is about so many things that are not acting. John allowed himself to look bad because he couldn't think fast enough. The agent asked for a monologue and John never stopped to think that he hadn't worked on that material for a long time. It never occurred to him to ask to come back. These are the things we learn over time. It's part of the "becoming" process of becoming an actor.

An actor who wants to be successful should have a monologue in his head, and a picture, resume and reel in his bag. You may only be new once, but you don't have to make the same mistake twice.

When I teach workshops, I notice that many young actors only want to get the agent and get the job and have an instant career. They want instant success before developing themselves and their craft. I tell all young actors: get in therapy, get into NYU, Yale, Juilliard, one of the League Schools.
– Jim Flynn, Jim Flynn, Inc.

Get decent headshots and a well-presented resume. Get Back Stage *and look for showcase work and whatever auditions you feel you are right for. Go to shows, movies, watch TV so that you know what's out there and what is current. Get a phone machine that works and get into the habit of checking your messages.*
– Dianne Busch, Leading Artists, Inc.

I think the philosophical basis is to work as much as possible, because the more you work, the more people have an opportunity to respond to it. Everyone in this business who is not an actor makes his living by recognizing talented actors.

The smartest thing a young playwright can do is to get to know a good, young, talented actor so that when there is a showcase of the playwright's play, he can recommend the actor. That's going to make his play look better. There are a number of stage directors in New York that, all they can really do (to be candid), is read a script and cast well and then stay out of the way. That can often be all you need.

Casting directors, agents, playwrights, directors, even stage managers are going to remember good actors. If they want to get ahead in their business, the more they remember good actors, the better off they're gonna be. Having your work out there is the crucial thing.

Studying is important because it keeps you ready. Nobody is going to give you six weeks to get your instrument ready. It's "here's the audition; do it now," so I believe in showcases. Actors tend to be too linear in their thinking. They think, "okay. I did this showcase and no agent came and nobody asked me to come to their office so it was a complete waste of time."

Well, I don't believe that. First of all, even a bad production is going to teach a young actor a lot of important things. Second of all, generally, if you do a good job in a play, it produces another job. Often it's in another showcase. Often, it's a year later, so if you're looking for direct links, you never see them.

What tends to happen is somebody calls you up and says, "I saw you in that show and you were terrific and would you like to come do this show?" It's like out of the blue, and it can take a long time. You may have to do eight great showcases or readings, but if your work is out there, there is an opportunity for people to get excited and if it isn't out there, then that opportunity doesn't exist. It doesn't matter how terrific you are in the office and how charming you are. None of that matters.
– Tim Angle, Manager, Shelter Entertainment Los Angeles

Show business is hard. Unless you are able to remain extremely focused and provide a personal life for yourself, you will have a difficult time dealing with the downs and ups of the lifestyle. Either get into therapy or start meditating; do whatever it takes to put your life in a healthy state.

If you are in an impossible relationship or if you have any kind of addiction problem, the business is only going to intensify it. Deal with these things first. If your life is in order, find a support group to help you keep it that way before you enter the fray.

People Who Need People
Life is easier with friends. Begin to build relationships with your peers.

There are those who say you should build friendships with people who already have what you want. I understand that thinking, but it's not my idea of a good time.

It's a lot easier to live on a shoestring and/or deal with constant rejection if your friends are going through the same thing. If your friend is starring on a television show or is king of commercials and has plenty of money while you are scrambling to pay the rent, it is going to be harder to keep perspective about where you are in the process. It takes different people differing amounts of time to make the journey. Having friends who understand that will make it easier for all of you.

Ruth Gordon's seventy year career included an Oscar for acting (*Rosemary's Baby*), Writers Guild Awards and several Oscar nominations for scriptwriting (*Pat and Mike, Inside Daisy Clover,* etc.). In her interview with Paul Rosenfield she had words of wisdom for us all.

Life is getting through the moment. The philosopher William James says to "cultivate the cheerful attitude." Now nobody had more trouble than he did except me. I had more trouble in my life than anybody. But your first big trouble can be a bonanza if you live through it. Get through the first trouble, you'll probably make it through the next one.
– The Los Angeles Times[6]

If you don't know anyone, get into a class or explore one of the 12-Step Support Groups. There's comfort for every problem from Alcoholics Anonymous to the other AA: Artists Anonymous. Even though this group is for all different kinds of artists, you'll find a majority are actors and writers.

There are other As: NA (Narcotics Anonymous), ACA (Adult Children of Alcoholics), OA (Overeaters Anonymous), etc. No matter who you are, there is probably a group with which you can identify that will provide you with confidential support for free.

You'll be better served if you don't look to these groups for your social life. The As supply a forum where you can talk about what is bothering you, but these groups are not your family and though helpful, they are not your best friends either.

Put energy into your personal relationships to fill those needs. You create your life. Will Rogers said, "people are about as happy as they want to be." I agree. I believe we all get what we really want.

If you are a member of SAG-AFTRA or Equity check out their support groups or join one of their committees. Being involved in a productive activity with your peers on a regular basis will give you a family and a focus – and might even lead to information about a job.

If you are fortunate and tenacious enough to find a job in the business, you'll find you are not only finally in the system, but you're also being paid to continue your education. There is no way in the world you can learn what it's really like to be in the business until you experience it firsthand. You'll spend every day with people who are interested in the same things you are. Who knows? You might not even like show business when you get a closer look. Better to find out now.

Get into an Acting Class

In order to find a good teacher, do some research. Who did he study with? What is the caliber of his students? Has this person worked professionally? You want someone whose advice is not theoretical. Work in class is totally different from actual professional work.

No one can teach you to act; a teacher can only stimulate your imagination and focus your work. Not everyone will be able to do that for you. Look for the teacher that will. Take the time to shop.

Teachers

If you are coaching for a particular part or audition, coaching one on one with a teacher can be a good idea if you can afford it. At a beginning stage of your career, however, it is important for you to interact with other actors so you can begin to practice one of the most important skills you'll ever need: the ability to get along with people both on and off stage. You'll also learn to evaluate the work of others and learn from their mistakes, as well as your own. Experiencing your peers tackling and solving the same problems you are facing will comfort you on many levels.

Here is a list of well-regarded teachers in New York. I know some personally and others were recommended by people whose judgment I trust.

JoAnna Beckson (joannabeckson.com) is one of the top ten coaches on both Disney Studios Acting Coaches List and The Actor's Studio Acting Coaches List. In *Backstage's* Poll of *Best of NYC*, JoAnna was the only woman on the list of four. 917-749-6922

William Esper Studio (esperstudio.com) was recently named to *The Hollywood Reporter's Top 25* list, but he has been a widely respected acting teacher and director with his own studio in NYC for over thirty-five years. He continues as director of the Professional Actor Training Programs at Mason Gross School of the Arts at Rutgers University since 1965. A graduate of the Neighborhood Playhouse School of Theatre, Esper trained as an actor and teacher with mentor Sanford Meisner, with whom he worked closely as a teacher and director for fifteen years.

Esper's list of amazing credits is lengthy and includes a juicy list of students from William Hurt to John Malkovich. 212-904-1350

I studied with Herbert Berghof at **HB Studios** (hbstudio.org) when I first came to New York. HB continues to be not only a rich resource for excellent teachers who are all working, but also offers classes that are extremely reasonable. You can check out prices online.

HB encourages you to audit many classes in order to find the teacher that is right for you. They offer classes seven days a week, during days and evenings. They define full-time study as seven classes per term. Until I checked the web page, I was unaware that HB offers a full array of classes and that full-time students can pursue classes six days a week and end up with a conservatory education. Whether you are looking for that or just a weekly acting, dance or musical class, HB is a respected place to study. F. Murray Abraham, Debbie Allen, Joy Behar,

Matthew Broderick, Billy Crystal, Clare Danes, Al Pacino, Geraldine Page are just a few of their illustrious alumni. 212-675-2370.

Terry Schreiber Studios (*tschreiber.org*) has an amazing staff including veteran *One Life to Live* director Peter Miner. Prices vary so check the website for information or 212-741-0209.

Karen Ludwig (kpludwig.com) is not only an actress with an impressive resume, she writes, directs, produces. She teaches MFA actors at The New School for Drama and at Westbeth Center for the Arts. Her class, "Word Is Out: Actors Write Their Own Stories for Solo Performance," is always in demand. She also teaches Intermediate-Advanced Scene Study at HB Studio.

Karen is one of the producers of *Uta Hagen's Acting Class/DVD*. Though no substitute for a class with Miss Hagen, it's still an amazing teaching tool available at amazon.com for $39.95. There is a nice interview with Karen on her webpage. 212-243-7570.

Allan Miller (allanmiller.org) lives in Los Angeles, but makes frequent trips to the city to teach. A member of The Actor's Studio, Allan is a gifted actor, director and teacher. Both his book *A Passion for Acting* and his videotape *Audition* are excellent. 818-907-6262.

Walker Clark (wcstudios.com) is a highly recommended coach for all ages, but is a particular favorite for kids (six and up) many of whom are currently on Broadway. He mostly teaches one-on-one, but does teach workshops 4 x a year. A former actor who hit on an effective technique for booking jobs that he calls "accessing the flow," this technique has been so popular, it's being adapted to other businesses. He charges $275 for an initial assessment of 80 minutes to two hours. He says that sometimes that's all people need. His popular book *The Cold Reading Conundrum* is available on his website. He teaches in New York, Los Angeles and San Diego.

LA based **Diane Hardin** (dianehardinacting.com) teaches regularly in New York. Her workshops for kids and young adults have aided Tony nominated actress Sydney Lucas (*Fun Home*), her brother Jake Lewis (*Newsies*) and many other working NY kids move to the next level.

Voice Teachers and Coaches

Juilliard educated **Badiene Magaziner** (voice-teacher.net) is one of the most highly regarded voice teachers in town with an impressive list of pupils currently starring on Broadway, in films and winning Grammys. An opera/operetta star before opening her own studio (read the touching story on her webpage), her pupils age from seven to 70. They can study either in her Manhattan, New Jersey studios or online. Her website blog has great guidelines for choosing a voice teacher as well as practicing tips.

Andrea Green's website (andreagreen.net) says that she is the teacher to whom directors and conductors send their performers, ENT doctors send their patients and current students send their colleagues. It's also the place where many agents send their clients of all ages. She has students in several shows on Broadway, is on the adjunct voice faculty of NYU, has been vocal consultant for Broadway shows and teaches Master Classes. Contact by email, andrea@andreagreen.net.

Vocal coach **Bob Marks** (bobmarks.com) has been preparing performers for auditions for 30 years. A musical arranger, conductor and Musical Director, Bob has an impressive list of Broadway and conservatory applicant success stories on his website. There are also several vocal warmups you might want to check out. Highly recommended for adults and children, Bob works six days a week teaching private sessions, workshops and masterclasses. His phone number is 212-365-4840, but he says email is best, bob@bobmarks.com.

Vocal coach **Michael Lavine's** website michaellavine.net doesn't have a lot of information in the formal sense; however, there are some helpful videos and his price is written clearly, I love that. Also highly recommended for all groups, he appears to be a rich source of inspiration in choosing material. Looks like the only way to contact him is via his "contact" button on his website.

Recommended Dance Studios

Dance studios recommended by many agents are **Broadway Dance Center** (bwydance.com), **Steps** (stepsnyc.com) and **Dance Molinari** (dancemolinari.com). Specific teachers with good reputations include Bam Bam, Drew, Soraya, Angel Feliciano, George Jones, Rhapsody, Kelly Peters. Many of these teachers teach at several studios.

If I have mentioned a studio with many teachers, know that all teachers are not equal. Check to see who the students are and audit to find the teacher that seems right for you. See at least three for comparison. In a good class you'll learn as much about yourself and the marketplace as you will about acting. If you're broke, see if you can work in exchange for tuition.

Showcases

Showcases offer visibility, experience and the ability to hone the most important skill of all: getting along with people. But choose your material carefully. Playing *King Lear* may give you great satisfaction and stretch you as an actor, but it doesn't present you in a castable light for anything other than a Shakespearean company.

I think they should try to find a showcase which presents them in a castable light, in a role that's appropriate, and that is convenient for agents to get to.

Before inviting agents, actors should try to get professional advice as to whether or not the project is worth inviting an agent to. You can engender hostility wasting an agent's evening if it's abominable.
– Phil Adelman, BRS/Gage Talent Agency

Be realistic in your expectations. You are probably not going to get an agent as a result of a showcase, but that director will direct another play or someone in the cast may recommend you for something else. You are growing, building your resume, maturing as an actor, and working your way into the system.

Analyzing the marketplace and using that information wisely can save you years of unfocused activity. If you were starting any other kind of business, you would expect to do extensive research to see if there was a need for the product you had decided to sell. In addition to checking out actors, note who is working and where, and keep a file on CDs, producers, directors, and writers.

Note which writers are writing parts for people like you. Learn and practice remembering the names of everybody. Know who the critics are. Note those whose taste agrees with yours. Think of this educational process as your Ph.D.

If you want to be a force in the business, begin to think of yourself as one and assume your rightful place. Synonyms of the word force inspire me: energy, power, strength, vigor, vitality, impact, value, weight.

Take your opportunities to grow. Your weight grows with every play you see, read, rehearse, and perform. You absorb energy from every interaction, so put yourself with artists you respect.

The Unions
Beginning actors unduly focus on membership in the unions. Although routinely one-third of the 180,000 SAG-AFTRA members make no money at all in a given year (and the numbers in Equity are similar), actors feel that membership in the unions will change their lives.

It will. It will make you ineligible to work in both the non-union films that could give you footage for your reel as well as the many non-union theatres across the land that would give you a chance to sharpen your acting tools.

Being in the union means you are a professional actor entitled to all its protections and privileges. I can remember the thrill when I got my Equity card (to me, that was the card that meant I was an actor), but I was far along in my resume before I joined. It makes sense to wait.

Union Wages
The term "quote" refers to the amount of money an actor will work for. We all start out at scale and after some luck and a few good roles, many

move up the scale to "double scale" or whatever the agent has been able to negotiate for. The quote has been built over time when the actor was in a position to negotiate. The highest fee you have been paid for a day/week, etc., becomes your quote.

It used to be that when an actor established a quote, a CD might call and ask the actor's quote and then ask to see him. These days having a quote means less and less, as CDs routinely call and say "we're paying SAG-AFTRA scale + 10%, take it or leave it."

What if there were no SAG-AFTRA scale? What would that actor be paid then? If you want a career, intend to live in a house, drive a car and have a family, you'll find that pretty difficult to do without residuals, health coverage and at least a minimum contract. You're not going to get that without union help. If you are a member of SAG-AFTRA, you do count; you are part of something. And people count on you.

Working as an Extra

While work as an extra gives you the opportunity to be on the set, unless you are looking for more extra work, I would not list it on the resume. You want any agent, producer, or casting director thinking of you for principal parts, so don't cloud his vision.

If you plan to be a career extra, working as an extra makes sense. If your goal is to play principal parts, why amass a resume that advertises you in a different capacity? It's tempting to accept extra work to qualify for guild membership, pay rent, keep insurance active or get on a set. I understand that.

I asked an agent if he had "John Smith" work as an extra, wouldn't casting directors and producers now only consider John to be an extra?

We all do. I spoke to a casting director the other day about an actor and that's exactly what she said. The actor has to learn where to draw the line and say, "okay, I can't do this anymore."
– Anonymous Agent

A lot of people can't. They get used to the money and the insurance and their resumes reflect that they are full-time extras. A credible agent might encourage actors to work as extras (after all, he is making a commission), but he expects them to know when to draw the line and stop doing extra work.

To me it's like saying, "here, these drugs will make you feel better. Just take them for a while, I know you will be able to stop in time."

If you are not ready to get work as a principal on a regular basis, it may not be time for you to be in the union. It would be more advantageous for you to work in some other capacity in order to pay your rent or to observe the business from the inside. Become an assistant or work in production. You will see what goes on, make some money and you won't be fooling yourself into thinking you are really acting. You will be more driven to pursue work that will further your career.

SAG-AFTRA and Equity both have financial assistance available to members in emergency situations. If you are not a member of a union, ask your acting teacher for advice.

There are also many city agencies equipped to deal with people in need. Low-cost counseling is available through both the city of New York and the schools of psychology of some universities. Call the schools or look online. A good start is The New York Counseling Center (nypcc.org).

Invaluable Actor Resources

Backstage newspaper and backstage.com provide invaluable stores of information about casting, classes and almost anything you have on your mind that involves showbusiness, particularly if you don't have representation. It's available at most newsstands and online.

Backstage still prints hard copy editions of their newspaper, but online subscriptions make the most sense because of the ability to instantly submit for the auditions they list regularly. *Backstage* also lists casting info at twitter.com/castingnyc.

Backstage warns that they don't vouch for the integrity of the people who invite you to audition. So use good sense and don't go to weird addresses in the dead of night. We've all read stories about actors, usually beautiful women, lured to their deaths by vague promises of jobs and/or connections. It's tempting to go to a producer's or director's home to read for something, but make sure these guys and their auditions are on the level before you set out. Be alert for anything iffy particularly those things that sound too good to be true. Don't go.

Though many agents and managers advise clients to use *Backstage* as an information source, they feel that advertising your picture or performances in anything but *Variety* or *Hollywood Reporter* is unproductive.

Backstage and *The Hollywood Reporter* are owned by Nederlander-based VNU. They also publish a stable of books about agents, managers, production companies, etc. as well as mailing labels for agents and managers.

Be careful about purchased mailing. Agents tell me when they see them, they know they are part of a mass mailing with no research involved and frequently just toss that mail.

Variety and *The Hollywood Reporter* have gone through vast changes over time. Both are dailies that publish showbiz information ranging from the grosses of the latest movies to actors' obituaries and who just got cast in what. There is much more agent information now, whose client just got cast, which actor switched representation and the latest on whichever agent has just defected from a prestigious agency with agents in tow.

To me, they've never been information sources for working or trying to work actors. There is no casting information as such, but each paper does run a weekly listing of current and preproduction of films and television product of every kind for networks and cable.

The Hollywood Reporter's annual Roundtable videos of actors, writers, directors and producers who are likely to be nominated in the next round of Oscar or Emmy voting are always informative and fun.

Though you can see a peek on *HR's* webpage, the videos are on Sundance TV titled *Closeup* and must be viewed there, at least initially.

Variety's version of the roundtable is called *The Contenders* and is available online as *Variety's Contender Conversations* at variety.com.

Though still important, both newspapers have competition now from deadline.com and other online publications.

The Hollywood Reporter's film production chart seems a little more comprehensive and easy to decipher than *Variety's*. Both papers are expensive subscriptions, but you can pick a copy up at any newsstand periodically or visit any library and read them for free online.

Actors Access (actorsaccess.com) is a free service allowing actors to post resumes, two pictures, contact information and for a price, video links. Their fee based service includes casting info and electronic self-submission via The Breakdown Services (breakdownservices.com).

The jobs posted are typically non-union or very small parts or a "when all else fails" plea that a casting director might release for general viewing. These breakdowns cover the country and are probably more valuable for actors outside the large entertainment centers.

There are fees per submission on Actors Access (actorsaccess.com) and for each download of sides from Showfax (showfax.com). An annual membership fee provides unlimited submissions and sides.

These two resources cover the entire United States as well as Vancouver and Toronto. I'd try the service for a while, paying each time until you establish this is something that works for you. You should find at least one job if you use these tools intelligently.

There are many websites where actors can upload their reels and publish their resume. The trick is to find the sites that buyers visit.

Three of my clients booked a Bollywood feature film recently from choreographers seeing their work at sceneinteractive.com. Actors and dancers can put up their reels online on this website and casting directors from all over the world see their work and directly book them.

– Thomas Scott, DDO Artists Agency

IMDb.com/IMDbPro.com

The Internet Movie Database was created in 1990 as an online database related to films and television. Begun by British movie-crazy engineer at Hewlett Packard, Col Needham, IMDb was originally his cottage hobby where the few people in the industry who knew about the site entered their own information. They still do, but now IMDb is the last word on credits, whether true or not.

That was then and this is now and what started out as a labor of love from a cinefile is now one of the 50 most popular websites in the world and Needham a powerful force in the business. He sold the business to Amazon in 1998, but retained leadership. *The Guardian* story (theguardian.com/film/2013/may/12/six-degrees-col-needham-imdb) is worth a read. IMDb is an indispensable free database with resources for everyone in the business.

Even more showbiz information is available for a fee ($19.99 monthly) at IMDbPro.com. The names, clients and staff of agencies, managers, production companies, publicists and distributors are there for your evaluation. You can get a free two week trial to see if it's helpful. You might not want/need it once you have representation, but having it for a couple of months for research would be worth it. I'll discuss this more when we are analyzing agents and their business.

The Power of IMDb and Twitter

I was startled to read that producers actually read IMDb's Starmeter for casting though having read it doesn't necessarily make it true.

...But perhaps the most remarkable thing about Needham's creation is that, by being the default destination for cinema-goers, he can now influence the movies made for their consumption. Costing $125 a year, IMDbPro provides fuller contact details for talent, as well as their upcoming projects; and, crucially, it boasts the Starmeter, which ranks actors, directors, writers and producers in order of desirability. The algorithm is simple: how many views has their profile page had that week? As Needham explains, the industry can use this info to invest wisely: "You can catch

a rising star while they're at cheaper prices, or you can find people who are still great but on the way down." Producers eager to cast the lead in Twilight *reportedly came up with Robert Pattinson by ordering a flunky to provide a list of everyone with a certain Starmeter rating who had also been in a Harry Potter film.*

– The Guardian[7]

Some young actors have told me that their agents demand a strong Twitter presence saying producers, directors and casting directors check your Twitter followers to see if you have some to bring with you should you be cast, but Michael Imbimbo doesn't agree:

I'm more concerned with using Social Media to get someone's work out there than how many followers they have. As I tell actors in seminars, the most important thing is to be a good actor.

– Michael Imbimbo, 9Muse

In Los Angeles, it can be a different story:

Your social media popularity does come into play when producers are deciding which talent to cast. It's not that difficult to understand why. I like to use a simple example when my clients ask me to explain this. Imagine you are a producer and you have a budget of $1,000 to cast an actor to play a somewhat insignificant role in your independent feature. Actor A has a social media following of two million and actor B has 500 followers. Let's assume that A and B are identical looking and have the same level of acting ability. As a producer, you know that actor A will post to Twitter, Facebook, Instagram, and Vine about their experiences working on the film. This means your film has the potential to reach two million more people, and they are more likely to go see the film because they are fans of the actor. This is like free advertising to one of your target demographics.

– Aur-Aelion Israel, Almond Talent Agency Los Angeles

The Internet Broadway Database (IBDb.com) is an online database of Broadway theatre productions operated by the Research Department of

The Broadway League. In addition to credits of Broadway shows from the 18th century until today, IBDb features links to musical cast recordings on iTunes, lists of awards and nominations, gross and attendance information.

Your Reference Library

At the beginning of my career I was fortunate to get a part in what turned out to be an Academy Award nominated film called *A Touch of Class*. The night I arrived on location in Marbella, I sat next to the wife of the writer-producer-director at a party honoring the cast.

Making conversation, and truly delighted to be involved with such a lovely script (Mel Frank eventually won an Oscar for it), I said to Ann Frank, "what a wonderful script. Is this Mel's first script?"

What did I know? I thought he was primarily a director and, as a New York actress, I was ignorant of things Hollywood. Ann was so cool. She neither walked away nor behaved in any way condescending. She just began patiently enumerating the edited version of her husband's incomparable credits.

It turned out that Mel was a famous Hollywood writer who with partner Norman Panama, had written the Bing Crosby-Bob Hope *Road* pictures plus many other classics. I was embarrassed but Ann was all class. She patted my arm and smiled, "this will be our little secret." All the time I was apologizing for my ignorance, I was promising myself that I would never be in that position again. These days with IMDb or IMDbPro, I check credits before every audition.

I also recommend your library be stocked with books that tell you what the business is really like (*Adventures in the Screen Trade, The Season, Final Cut,* etc.), as well as biographies of successful people of every kind that will provide role models in your quest for achievement. Here is a list that will give your library a good start:

Aaron Spelling: a primetime life/Aaron Spelling
Adventures in the Screen Trade/William Goldman

Audition/Michael Shurtleff

The Complete Directory to Primetime Network TV Shows
    Tim Brooks & Earle Marsh

The Devil's Candy/Julie Salamon

Equity Agency Regulations

The Film Encyclopedia/Ephraim Katz

The Filmgoer's Companion/Leslie Halliwell

Final Cut/Steven Bach

How I Made 100 Films in Hollywood and Never Lost a Dime/Roger Corman

How to Sell Yourself As An Actor/K Callan

Hype & Glory/William Goldman

Indecent Exposure/David McClintock

The Empty Space: A Book About the Theatre:
Deadly, Holy, Rough, Immediate/Peter Brook

The Last Great Ride/Brandon Tartikoff

The Los Angeles Agent Book/K Callan

Making Movies/Sydney Lumet

Monster/John Gregory Dunne & Joan Didion

My Lives/Roseanne

The New York Agent Book/K Callan

On Directing Herald Clurman

On the Technique of Acting/Michael Chekhov

Ovitz/Robert Slater

Rebel Without a Crew/Robert Rodriquez

Reel Power/Mark Litwak

Sanford Meisner on Acting/Sanford Meisner

Saturday Night Live/Doug Hall & Jeff Weingrad

Screen World/John Willis

The Season/William Goldman

Theatre World/John Willis

TV Movies/Leonard Maltin

Ultimate Film Festival Survival Guide/Chris Gore

You'll Never Eat Lunch in this Town Again/Julia Phillips

Wake Me When It's Funny/Garry Marshall
Who's Who in the Motion Picture Industry/Rodman Gregg
Who's Who in American Film Now/James Monaco
Wired/Bob Woodward

If you know of any other books that belong on this list, let me know and I'll include them in subsequent editions. I consider books like *Wired, Indecent Exposure* and *Saturday Night Live* to be instructive and realistic about the business. I keep them on my bookshelf to keep my values in perspective. I want to remember how easy it is to get caught up in the glamour, publicity, money and power of this fairytale business. I want to remember that those things leave as quickly as they come.

I need these books to remind me why I got into the business in the first place. I have to strive to remember that success doesn't fix you. It may make you feel better for a while, but you're always you, just with a different set of problems.

I cannot stress strongly enough the need for a good reference library. For fun, read Tony Randall's book *Which Reminds Me*. For inspiration, Carol Burnett's *One More Time*. Judd Apatow's *Sick in the Head* is a must for comedy folk. To gain insight on how to get into and what goes on at film festivals, read Chris Gore's *The Ultimate Film Festival Guide*. Roseanne's book, *My Lives*, speaks candidly of the behind-the-scenes intrigue involved with her show. It's instructive.

Breakdown Services

Back in the day, agents in Hollywood journeyed to each studio every day to read the latest script, make notes, and submit actors. Gary Marsh was one of those readers, doing the job for his agent mother. He changed the system forever when he called the studios and said something like, "if you give me all your scripts, I will summarize them and make a list of the types of actors needed for the parts, the size of each role, etc., and provide that information to all the agents. This will be better for everyone. You won't have those people in your offices and they won't have to drive." Thus Breakdown Services was born.

The much-maligned service costs agents and managers a hefty amount. Though they must agree not to show it to actors, some actors get their hands on it anyway.

Whether or not it's a good idea to have access to the Breakdown is debatable. Casting directors already don't have enough time to look at all the agents' submissions. How will they ever open all the actors' envelopes, much less consider what's inside?

It's just plain counterproductive for the most part [when actors get their hands on the Breakdown]. The casting directors are likely ignoring submissions from non-represented actors. And as far as represented actors go, you better hope you're wasting your agents' office time pointing out what you're right for. Our work is about everything after (and hopefully before) the Breakdown. We continue to talk to casting and find out so much. Often they want a name for a part or are just looking for back-up ideas if their offer falls through or change their mind about the "specs" after the first round of auditions or cut the part or a myriad of other factors.

Casting is an activity and that means change, give-and-take, and yes mistakes happen. For an actor to pin his expectations to the snapshot in time of a Breakdown is wrong. Our office's response to an actor quoting Breakdowns is "that's not a mail-order catalogue there."
– Jay Kane, Talentworks New York

Whereas some actors are able to use the purloined information intelligently, others merely manage to alienate their agents. Though invaluable, the Breakdown doesn't include everything. Many roles aren't listed unless the casting director needs an unusual actor for a role. More times than not, the audition will be filled with actors from producer requests, not from submissions. Since not everything comes out in the Breakdown, it is important to assess your agent's other contacts. If your agent doesn't have access to information other than The Breakdown, that's still a lot of information if he uses it wisely.

Stumbling and Physics

You're not going to be perfect when you begin. It's part of the physics of life that you have to stumble a bit to find your way. My research of people and careers (including my own) leads me to conclude that there is a three year stumble rule, so don't give yourself a bad time for not having things together immediately. One just has to be green for a while before you can season and grow.

It's physics, a law of life.

So move in, get settled and begin your stumble.

Wrap Up

Tools for First Agent
- ✓ support group
- ✓ decent credits
- ✓ open calls
- ✓ audition DVD/electronic sample of your work
- ✓ focus
- ✓ entrepreneurial skills
- ✓ integrity
- ✓ fellow actors
- ✓ growth – three year stumble
- ✓ marketable product

Personal Resources
- ✓ family
- ✓ teachers
- ✓ friends

Professional Resources
- ✓ job in business
- ✓ acting class/teachers
- ✓ theatrical publications

Reference Library
- ✓ educational
- ✓ inspirational
- ✓ indispensable

Breakdown Services
- ✓ important tool for agents
- ✓ can be self-destructive in the hands of the wrong actor

chapter _7

Self-Knowledge

Before you can sell yourself to the marketplace, you must identity what you have to offer. A reader emailed that she sent her picture and resume to many agents and though many asked to meet her, no one would sign her. I asked her to send me her picture. She was an adorable sunny Rachel McAdams type. I could understand why everyone had wanted to meet her.

I studied the pictures trying to figure out why all these agents passed after asking to meet her. I wondered what didn't match. Finally I asked if by chance she had an "edge," if she was more Angelina Jolie than Rachel McAdams? When she answered affirmatively, I knew we had identified the problem. All the agents who asked to see her obviously had room on their lists for Rachel but not for Angelina. Once the actress adjusted the picture to match her personality, a whole different group of agents responded and she was quickly signed.

Actors need to] be aware of their strongest gift and concentrate on it.
— Diana Doussant, Leading Artists, Inc.

When an actor comes into our office, we only have what he tells us to go on, to teach us how to sell them. The headshot, the resume, the material the actor chooses for his showcase all tell us whether or not the actor knows what he has to sell. If the elements don't all line up, there is a disconnect and we can't sell that.
— Jed Abrahams, Kazarian, Measures, Ruskin & Associates

Before you start meeting people, you need to find an image to present. Check to see what the demand is and where you fit in.
— Ann Steele, Ann Steele Agency

Be the best person you can be. Learn about yourself. You need a solid center to deal with life when things get tough. You have to know what your bottom line is and what you are willing to sacrifice in order to get what you want.
– Jack Menasche, Independent Artists Agency, Inc.

Be aware of where you fit into the marketplace and if you don't know now, you might one day. Most importantly, if there is anything else you can see yourself doing with your life, do it. This business is very tough and you have to want it more than anything else in your life in order to stick with it.
– Diana Doussant, Leading Artists, Inc.

Acting class is a good place to start the investigation into your persona. Ask your teacher to suggest some material for you. That choice will give you an idea how the teacher sees you. If you tackle a variety of characters, you'll soon get a feeling for the material that resonates within you. You'll see what begins to feel right. My first teacher, Herbert Berghof, encouraged us to explore playwrights from our own part of the country.

Do you have the right talents?
When people use the word talent in relation to actors, they usually refer to acting talent, but other talents govern how effective the acting talent can be. Once you reach a certain level, all your competition is terrific. Any one actor sitting in the audition waiting room would be a good choice. The talent to self-motivate, focus, maintain balance and one's own voice under pressure will be the deciding factor in who prevails. The late agent Archer King agrees:

Talent has never been enough. Talent never will be enough. You have to have commitment and a singular purpose. Every decision has to be a career decision.

When you hear about the thousands of starving actors vying for five agents and one part, you can screen out many of those thousands. They won't be your competition because they have no appetite for taking care of business. It doesn't matter if there are only five agents and one part, as long as you get the part and one of the agents.

I asked agents to name the most important single piece of advice they would like to give to actors. Almost everyone gave some version of the same answer, "know which one you are."

Don't expect to play Anna Kendrick's parts if you look like Rebel Wilson. When I first arrived in New York, I did everything I could lest I be mistaken for the middle-class lady from Texas I was. I wanted to be a sophisticated New Yorker.

What I didn't realize, Texas accent notwithstanding, was that my very middle-classness is what I had to sell. I have played women who went to Vassar, but more often buyers can and will get someone for those parts who actually went to Vassar .

I'm an authentic lady from Texas who has raised three children and had various life experiences that continue informing my persona.

You must find a way to look at yourself with clarity and notice all your talents. There is nobody else with your particular components. You must become aware of what is uniquely you and find a way to amplify and use that energy to a universality of the life experience.

H. Shep Pamplin has retired from agenting and now teaches and runs a theatre in Oklahoma, but he was wise:

I personally believe that anyone who comes into this business has one point where they can enter the business: literally a skill, a qualification, that will get them a job tomorrow.

If they are willing to take the time to find out what it is and go for that area, they can get hired, they can start working. And then they can begin to explore the other areas that they might not yet be prepared for.

There are certain qualifications that are required in every area. People who want to do musical theatre have to be able to sing and dance. They need to take the classes. They must do regional theatre and work their way up, just like in corporate

America. Those who want to do film and TV, other than those soap beauties who land a job just on their looks, you have to have certain qualifications.

Whatever area you are strongest in, you should go for that first. Then when you are making money in the business, you interview better and you audition better. You meet people better when you are working in the business than when you are a waiter or a waitress trying to get just any job. You're going for film, you're going for commercials, you're going for television, and just grabbing for everything rather than learning to focus and say, "where can I get hired today?"

Once you are working in the business, then you can move your way through the path you want to be on. That's the client I like to work with. One that is already at this point and we can move you from here to here to here and take you to where you want to be. Then you are a goal-oriented career-driven client.

– H. Shep Pamplin

Actors need to be in touch with who they are, their type, their strengths and weaknesses. They need an ability to grasp the fact that they can't be seen for everything in town and that just because a friend gets an appointment doesn't mean he will get one too. Actors have to figure out what they are right for and what they are best at; they need to know their own limitations.

– Gary Krasny, The Krasny Office

Many young actors are celebrity wannabes. They're not process oriented. They're not working on their craft. They're not working on who they are and what they do and making that the best, bringing the life to it.

They're more goal oriented and looking just to get the job. Unless you have the training, that one job you get is going to be a flash in the pan. After that, that actor's career is over unless they have a good solid foundation of training.

– Jim Flynn, Jim Flynn, Inc.

A lot of people are just totally unrealistic. They're either young and unattractive and/or overweight, and inexperienced. And they do have a chance of being an actor, but when you look like that, it's not going to happen for twenty or twenty-five years.

They'll have to be a character person. They have a fantasy of acting and they haven't done anything about it. They must do the work, they must learn the craft.
– Lionel Larner, Lionel Larner Ltd.

A friend of mine struggled when she first came to Los Angeles. I tried to help her by suggesting a part in a show I was doing. Mary was a young pretty actress with great comic gifts. The part was the town bad girl. She said, "you obviously don't know who I am. I have no breasts. No one will ever cast me in a part like that."

She wasn't whining, just stating a fact. When she got her break, it was playing an upper crust young lady born with a silver spoon in her mouth. The clarity with which she was able to see herself gave her a focus on and offstage that won her an integral part in a hit show.

It's Your Machine

In an interview, Sigourney Weaver quoted George Wolfe's speech to graduates of NYU's Tisch School for the Arts:

He said early on he'd written this musical called Paradise *and he'd had great hopes for it. And the day it opened was the day it closed. He looked out at all the students and said, "I'm going to tell you what your greatest teacher is, and the greatest creative tool you have in your career. It's failure. Failure will teach you all these things that you need to know."*

He said, "It's like standing in a huge casino and everyone has a slot-machine. And you're feeding your slot machine and nothing is happening and all around you people are hitting the jackpot and getting all this stuff. And you're going, 'Well, I want to go over there to that machine. It's obviously a better machine than mine.'
"But," he said, "stick with your own machine. It may take you longer. But when you hit, you're still yourself."
– Back Stage West[8]

Actors make a big mistake when they turn over their power to everybody else, making it about everybody else. Actors have to be very clear about who they are and what choices they are going to make when they go into auditions, and, if it's not working, to change their direction. You can't blame it on everybody else.

Actors don't understand how the business works. I can't really blame them. All they want to do is act and everything seems to get in the way of doing their piece. I feel bad about that. They don't understand the reality of what it takes to mount a project, the amount of money involved, the fact that everybody involved is scared to death for their lives, their reputations, and that when somebody comes walking through the door, they better be less scared than these people are or they're not going to get the job. Nobody's going to trust them with the money and the responsibilities that go with some of the roles.

– Marvin Starkman, Producer

Sometimes we do get the idea that insecurity is charming and that admitting it is even endearing. We announce to buyers at an audition that we are petrified of being there and that we are sure we won't do our best. Really? When had you planned to do your best? In front of 5,000 people? Will that be easier? Insecurity is not charming. It is not appealing. It is not endearing. And it is certainly not going to inspire the people with money to trust you with the responsibility of carrying their project.

If you find yourself in a continuing state of anxiety, there is either something physiologically wrong with you or you are getting off on it.

If you enjoy being a basket case, take responsibility for that. This can be a marketable attribute if you prepare yourself to play those kinds of roles. Otherwise, get yourself together and start behaving as though you have complete confidence in your abilities. Pretty soon, you won't be pretending anymore.

All we have is now. If you are not fulfilled by the now, get out of the business. If the payoff for you is the big bucks, the Tony, the Oscar or the Emmy, change jobs now. You will miss your whole life waiting for the prize. If you are unlucky enough to get the prize with this mindset, you will find you are just the same unhappy person that you were the day before, but now you have an Oscar.

Mental health, balance and self-esteem are essential.

The late Barry Douglas from DGRW was articulate in his analysis of the actor's self-confidence:

The most important person to like you is the audience. Before the audience can like you, the producer has to agree to pay your salary. Before the producer agrees to pay your salary, the director has to agree to work with you.

Before the director can agree to work with you, odds are, the casting director has to bring you in and say you're right for the role. Before the casting director can say you're right for the role, an agent has to submit you. Before any of these people get to see you, the first person who has to say, "I'm good," is the actor.

You've got to be confident enough to take a risk with a piece of material, to look at a piece and say, "ah, I can expose the humanity of this character; I can develop the creativity of this moment of the theatre or film or television better than anyone in the universe. I am the first person on this." If the actor doesn't believe that, no one else will. It's got to come from the actor first. The actor who is too insecure to ask for an agent just might not make it.

– Barry Douglas

Reality

In a fantasy business, it's a constant struggle to maintain perspective and remain excruciatingly realistic. You must realize that everybody's career is different. Someone may be twenty-five years old and be a star and then another actor may not make a dime until they are fifty. It's a sign of maturity to be able to enjoy the process and not be concerned with other people's idea of success. So your friend is working at Long Wharf and you're doing off-Broadway, everybody's career is different.

It's a business of survival. Your turn will come if you're good. It may not come as often as it should, but it'll come. They will eventually find you. You can make it if you can survive and you can only survive if you have no choice.

Some go into the business saying, "Well, I'll do this for five years and I'll see what it's like or I'll do something else." If you have something else you can happily

do, do it. It's only the people who are so committed, so desperate in some way that they'll put up with the humiliation, that they will allow themselves on ten minutes notice to be there, they'll allow themselves to be open and vulnerable; to still expose who they are and still be strong and protected enough to survive that kind of open wound life, they're the only ones who are going to make it, the people who have no choice.
– Barry Douglas

Continuing the *Back Stage West* interview Sigourney Weaver says:

You know, Meryl Streep was at school with me. And she was obviously ready for success more than nerdy me, at least. And it was hard, because she went right from Yale into Lincoln Center with no showcases at all. But I've learned that everyone has their own timetable and that's just the way it is. Everyone has their own path. It may not be the path you want, but in the end it's better for you.
– Back Stage West[9]

This is a business that rightfully or wrongfully, prefers prettier people. The prettier person gets the second look. It's a reflection of what the audience wants.
– Tim Angle, Manager, Shelter Entertainment Los Angeles

The late Fifi Oscard had these words of wisdom:

I believe you will arrive at the success point you are intended to arrive at simply by working hard, not faltering, and having confidence that it does happen. It does happen. You get where you're supposed to get in our business.
– Fifi Oscard

Don't look at other actors' careers from the wrong end of the telescope. Don't look at what they did and think, "oh, they just went from one thing to the next. It was just this inevitable golden path and they just had to walk along it."
– Tim Angle, Manager Shelter Entertainment Los Angeles

Just because you don't get the job doesn't mean you're not good.

There are variables you can't control. You can't expect any kind of time table as to when you can work. That is not the actor's life.

While you are paying your dues, you might get a job that gives you visibility and money for a month or even a year or two that makes you think you are further along in the process than you are.

Once your series (only one job, after all, no matter how long it lasts) or movie or play is over, you are not visible in that show business way and may think your career is over since your employment opportunities are no longer high profile.

Visibility is a double-edged sword. In television especially, the buyer may prefer a talented new face over an actor who has just finished a series. Frequently a semi-famous face finds itself unemployed because the buyer thinks it's too identifiable with a previous show.

Consistent Work

The task that takes more time than anything else is looking for and winning the work. Even two-time Academy Award winner Sally Field had her ups and downs. She says it isn't like she thought it would be. She's constantly reading scripts and creating opportunities for herself. When things weren't happening in films, she went to Broadway starring in *The Goat.* After her brilliant Emmy winning performances on ABC's *Brothers and Sisters,* she started reading all those scripts again and landed another Oscar nomination for her performance in *Lincoln.*

That's depressing and comforting at the same time: If even Sally Field has to scramble, who am I to complain? I think sometimes that the most appealing part of the business may just be that the chase is never over. Maybe if they just gave me all the jobs, I might lose interest and leave the business. Yeah, right.

Assess Yourself & the Marketplace

Are you a young character person? A juvenile? Someone who is right for a soap? To see yourself clearly within the framework of the business, study the marketplace. View theatre, television, and film with distance.

Notice what kinds of actors consistently work, not *which, but* what *kind.*
What is common to the people that work? Who is like you and who
isn't? Make a list of recent performances you realistically think you
would have been right for. Ask your agent if he agrees.

As you become informed about the business, you will begin to
perceive the essence of people and notice its role in the casting process.
More important than the look is essence. The thing that is the same in
the many diverse roles of Robert De Niro is the strength of spirit.

RandyHiller who casts at Disney told an Austin audience at SXSW,

*...few actors could be so versatile that they become entirely different people, and that
most essentially play versions of themselves – or, as she put it, they "operate on the
same base energy sphere". She said some, like Sean Penn, could expand the
parameters widely.*

*As an example, she said that Kevin Spacey "is not particularly warm" and
would be unlikely to be cast in an avuncular role.*
– The Guardian[10]

Think like a casting director. Consider Matt Damon, Jim Carrey,
Frances McDormand. What is their essence? Cast them in other
people's roles. How would Melissa McCarthy's part in *Spy* have been if
Tina Fey had played it? What if Jeremy Pivens had played Paul
Giamatti's part in *Love and Mercy?* Thinking like a casting director will
help you understand why you will never be cast in certain roles and why
no one else will be cast in your parts.

*...actors should take comfort from the fact that there are many variables that come
into play before acting talent becomes a deciding factor in whether or not an actor got
a particular part. Acting talent, [Disney, casting director Randy Hiller said] may
only account for 7% of the reason a particular actor would be cast in a role, citing
other factors ranging from age and ethnicity to "box office value in China".*
– Ibid. [11]

Does your appearance match your essence? As Tim Angle said, the business gravitates toward prettier people. Just as in life. Getting upset about that fact is like being upset because the sun shines in your window every morning and wakes you up. Get a shade. If you are not pretty, be clever.

In dark moments I read Ruth Gordon's words:

Two things first. Beauty and courage. These are the two most admired things in life. Beauty is Vivien Leigh, Garbo; you fall down in front of them. You don't have it? Get courage. It's what we're all in awe of. It's the New York Mets saying, "we'll make our own luck." I got courage because I was five-foot-nothing and not showgirl-beautiful. Very few beauties are great actresses.
– Los Angeles Times[12]

The Process

Nobody changes the rules. What you can do is play the game for what you want or at least toward your ends. Nobody will force you to do work that you find insulting or demeaning. You have to figure out the rules in order to figure out how to play the game. You have to figure out what is a variable and what's not.

If actors would take the time to put themselves in the shoes of the people they're dealing with, they would very quickly figure out what's reasonable and what's not. Actors don't understand why Equity Principal Auditions are a bad idea.

The reason is that no one can look at 250 people auditioning in a single day and give an accurate response. That's one of the reasons they only see forty people for a role. Knowing that isn't going to make your life easier, but it means it's not some arbitrary system where God touches this person and says, "you get to audition," and you, as the untouched person, sit there wondering. If you think about a director casting a play and you understand what he has to do to cast it as well as possible, at least you know what you're up against. It's not some vague, amorphous obstacle. It's not fair but at least it makes sense.

What you know is never as bad as your imagination. If you know what you're up against, it can be difficult, but at least it's concrete. What you don't know, your imagination turns into, "everyone in the business knows I shouldn't be doing this.

I'm just not talented." It's like conspiracy theories.
– Tim Angle, Manager Shelter Entertainment Los Angeles

When Sigourney Weaver was a young girl, her father ran NBC. When he left there and tried to start a fourth network, he received death threats and subsequently lost everything. Weaver says,

...From my father, I learned that business was not fair. I knew that things did not happen in any kind of logical, nice way. I didn't believe that people necessarily got what they deserved. Knowing that the business was unfair helped me.
– Back Stage West[13]

We'd all be a lot better off if actors knew what went on behind the agent's door. There's not much mystery about what happens between the agent and the casting director and the director and the producer, as a lot of actors want to weave myths about. Most of the time, the actor is just not right for the part.
– Kenneth Kaplan, The Gersh Agency

Careers are like pyramids. You have to build a very solid base. It takes a long time to do it and then you work your way up. No single decision makes or breaks a career. I don't think actors are ever in a position where it's the fork in the road or the road not taken, where it's, "okay, your career is now irrevocably on this course. Too bad, you could have had that."

If an actor looks at another person's career and says, "I don't want that," he doesn't have to have it. People do what they want to do. It's like people who are on soaps for twenty years. Well, it's a darn good job, pays you a lot of money and if you're really happy, great. But if you're an actor who doesn't want to do that, you won't. Nobody makes you sign a contract. Again. And again. And again.

Every decision you make is a risk because it's all collaborative and it can all stink. Every play at the Public is not a good play. Not every television series is a piece of junk. People make decisions based on what price they want to pay, because there is a price.

If you don't want to work in television, there's a price. If you want to work in

television, there's a price. If you want to work in New York in theatre, there's a price. You have to decide if that's worth it; it's an individual decision, not a moral choice. It shouldn't be something you have to justify to anybody but yourself.

It's not about proving to your friends that you're an artist. It's about what's important to you at that moment. People can do two years on a soap and that can give them enough money to do five years of theatre. And that's pretty important. It depends on why you're doing it and what you're looking to get out of it. What is the big picture? Nobody knows it but you.

– Tim Angle, Manager Shelter Entertainment Los Angeles

Jerry Kahn has retired now, but his words are still relevant:

One of the things I wish actors knew about was the business part of the business. A little bit more about their union rules and regulations so that every time you get an actor a job you don't have to explain to them what the contract entails. That information is as readily available to them as it is to the agent. It's irritating to have to go through all that when you book somebody.

– Jerry Kahn

Being Smart

One of the most candid and entertaining people I ever met was the late agent Beverly Anderson who said her best advice is,

Be smart. Don't be naive. If you're not smart, it doesn't make any difference how much talent you have or how beautiful you are. You're dead. In all my experience of thirty-nine years, of all the people that I can sit here and say, "They made it," they did not make it because they were the most talented or the most beautiful or even the best organized or the most driven. They made it because they were basically extremely smart human beings.

It has nothing to do with the best looks and the best talents, the best voice or the best tap-dancing ability. It's being smart. Donna Mills is smart. Alan Alda is smart. Johnny Carson is smart. Barbara Walters is smart. They made it because they're smart, not because of talent. Talent is just automatic in this business.

Who's to say that Barbra Streisand has the best voice in the world? I mean, let's face it, she sings well and has gorgeous styling and she makes a great sound, but who's to say if she has the best voice? I think the one ingredient that counts the most in this business is "smarts." You could be talented and be sucked in by some agent who signs you up and never sends you out and you sit there for five years and say, "well, I thought they were going to get me a job." Is that smart? To be smart is the best thing. Talent is a dime a dozen.

– Beverly Anderson

Part of being smart is factoring in what your dream may cost. When he was working on *The X-Files*, David Duchovny underscored a reality I have witnessed firsthand:

"I'm OK, I can take care of myself, but I feel isolated and lonely. I'm not happy. If I knew what it was going to be like, would I have taken the series? Can I also know what it would have been like if I didn't take the series?

I hate those kinds of things, where people say, 'Stop bitching, you could be working at Burger King now.' As if those are the only two options for me, either act, or "would you like a soda with your fries?" But doing a television show is like riding an elephant: it goes where it wants, with or without your say. Does that make me an ungrateful bastard?"

– Movieline[14]

Visionary Buckminster Fuller says it's a law of physics that if you take all the wealth in the world and redistribute it equally, in a hundred years (or fifty or whenever), the distribution will return to what it is today. Some people work hard, some don't. Some save. Some squander. Them that has, gets; them that don't, won't.

It's up to you and how smart you are: whether you make positive choices; whether you choose to walk away at the first sign of negative thinking; how well you know which one you are. You will have just what you want.

Isn't that nice? It's all in your hands.

Wrap Up

Analyze
- ✓ how the business works
- ✓ who gets hired
- ✓ who hires and why
- ✓ which actor is getting your parts
- ✓ what do they have that you don't have
- ✓ your strengths
- ✓ your weaknesses

Important
- ✓ focus on the process not the goal
- ✓ study
- ✓ nourish your talent
- ✓ be organized
- ✓ acquire business skills
- ✓ be smart

chapter 8

What Everybody Wants

If you could sign with any agent in town, who would you choose?
Would WME be right for you? Could BRS/Gage be the answer? Maybe
The Gersh Agency? These agencies are all prestigious, but that doesn't
necessarily mean selecting A instead of B would be the wise career
move. Before we look for the ultimate agent or agents, consider what
agents are looking for.

The Definitive Client

*I want to know either that they work and make a lot of money so I can support my
office, or that the potential to make money is there. I am one of the people who goes
for talent, so I do take people who are not big money-makers, because I am impressed
by talent.*
– Martin Gage, BRS/Gage Talent Agency

I love the late Beverly Anderson's story about Sigourney Weaver:

*She floated in and she did something no one had ever done. She had this big book
with all her pictures from Bryn Mawr or Radcliffe of things she had done. She
opened this book and she comes around and drapes herself over my shoulders from
behind my chair and points to herself in these pictures. She was hovering over me and
I thought, "No matter what happens with me, this woman is going to make it." There
was determination and strength and self-confidence and positiveness.*
– Beverly Anderson

Part of Weaver's strength comes from having a strong, successful
father/role model, Pat Weaver, producer of *The Today Show*, and another
valuable asset: a top-drawer education.

One of New York's most insightful and successful agents, the late Michael Kingman, was articulate about what drew him to an actor:

His talent. To be moved. To laugh. Feelings. Somebody who has contagious emotions. I'm looking for actors with talent and health, mental health and the ability to say, "it's my career and I devote my life to this." It's an attitude, not a spoken thing. It's an attitude that says, "today is not the last day of my life."
— Michael Kingman

Geez, if we had mental health, would we need to be actors?

We're not afraid to do the heavy lifting when it comes to developing talent. Many companies are looking for your general leading man and woman and so are we, but we also look for and foster unique talents that may not fit in a particular mold. If we meet someone with tremendous talent and confidence, even though they are green in the business, we don't mind guiding them, suggesting teachers, formatting their resumes to the industry standard and making sure they get great pictures so their unique talents will get noticed by casting directors.
— Renee Glicker, About Artists Agency

We are always looking for young people age fifteen to twenty-five who are savvy about the biz and have poise and talent. Good looks are extremely important to our TV and film contacts, so we are forced to make that important too.
— Dianne Busch, Leading Artists, Inc.

The people we work with best are actors who are committed to their craft and are willing to do regional theatre as well as off-Broadway and Broadway as well as film and television. The focus should be on training and growing yourself. Experiencing life so you can bring that to a character and to a performance. The interview part of the audition is just as important as the audition. Who you are as a person, as well as who you are as an actor.
— Jim Flynn, Jim Flynn, Inc.

Actress Laurie Walton was an agent for a while. She said her perspective totally changed when she became an agent:

It's really difficult to turn down actors. Old friends need an agent. I want to help them all out, but when my boss holds that picture up in front of my face and says, "are you ready to make a phone call to Jay Binder and ask him to see this client?" That puts things more in perspective. And actors don't understand that I don't make the sole decision.
— Laurie Walton

I look for preparedness, humor — about the process of looking for work — thick-skin (unfortunately).
— Jay Kane, Talentworks New York.

The things that attract me are the sense of self as an actor, sense of humor, being prepared, taking responsibility for themselves and their work.
— Diana Doussant, Leading Artists, Inc.

I want clients to come to me prepared, to have a sense of who they are, the kind of career they're likely to have, good self-knowledge, good reality about themselves.
— Phil Adelman, BRS/Gage Talent Agency

If they're older and have been in the business and don't have some career going, it's harder because they're now going to be up against people who have many more important credits.
— Robert Malcolm, The Artists Group

Since I am my own boss, I can choose who I want to work with. When a client approaches and I get even an inkling that this is going to be a high-maintenance client, I don't choose him.
— Jim Flynn, Jim Flynn, Inc.

Actors need to know themselves and what they have to sell. If you are a character actor, embrace it. Don't try to see yourself as the ingenue or the leading man if you're not. I've had actors come in telling me that they are very funny. Then, they sing a song to showcase their pretty voice instead of the comedic talent that will make them stars. I'll frequently tell an actor to go home and learn three new songs that showcase their comedy skills.

— Jed Abrahams, Kazarian, Measures, Ruskin & Associates

I think it's important for an actor to be able to adjust to auditioning being their main job. Their goal has to be to do a great audition and then let it go. If they book the job, that's the cherry on top.

— Renee Glicker, About Artists Agency

What to Look for in an Agent

Schools sometimes give students a laundry list of questions to ask agents that the actors ask without even knowing why they ask them. When I meet an actor, I want to have a conversation with him out of which questions come.

I think actors should have an idea of what they want to hire because they are hiring the agent. If I were an actor, I'd want to know that the agent and I were on the same page about the kinds of projects he would be interested in submitting me for. I'd want to know the agent's perception of my ability.

The art of communication is extremely important. You have to imagine that apart from your lover, family, boyfriend, this is the person you are going to speak to more often than your mother and you have to not be intimidated to pick up the phone and have a conversation. Is that agent someone I want to talk to?

— Jim Wilhelm, DGRW

Busy Work?

Be practical in your assessment of auditions. Actors sometime grade their agents by the number of auditions they generate, not the quality or appropriateness. If you're not being sent on projects that you are right for, all those auditions are just for show. Producer and former agent Marvin Starkman has a realistic perspective:

If the actor/agent relationship were based on getting auditions for everything, then the agent would have a right to say that you must get everything he sends you out on. If you don't get everything he sends you on, then you have a one-sided relationship.
– Marvin Starkman

Ouch! Of course, that's predicated on his getting you out on everything in town. But still, his point is well taken. Neither actor not agent is going to score every time.

Vision/Goals
The actor and agent need to be on the same wavelength:

I had a funny looking lady come in, mid thirties, chubby, not very pretty. For all I know, this woman could be brilliant. I asked her what roles she could play, what she thought she should get. She saw herself playing Gwyneth Paltrow's roles.

I could have been potentially interested in this woman in the areas in which she could work. But it was a turnoff, because not only do I know that she's not going after the right things so she's not preparing correctly, but she's not going to be happy with the kinds of things I'm going to be able to do for her. So I wouldn't want to commit to that person.
– Phil Adelman, BRS/Gage Talent Agency

Size
A key aspect to consider in overall agent effectiveness is size. When we speak of size in relation to an agent, we are speaking of his client list: the number of actors the agent has committed to represent exclusively.

One person can't effectively represent a hundred people. It's like going to the store and buying everything you see. You can't possibly use it all, you're just taking it out of circulation. There are some agents who may sign you just to protect their client who is in your category.

It might feed your ego to be signed ("I have an agent!"), but if you are not signed with a credible agent that you can trust, you may just be taking yourself out of the marketplace.

Better to wait until you have the credits to support getting a better agent than to sign with someone who can't represent you effectively. Many agents believe a good ratio is one agent to twenty to twenty-five clients. An agency with four agents can do well by a hundred or even a hundred and forty clients, but that really is the limit.

Or it used to be the limit. More and more agencies are loading up their list with far more clients than they can handle. For one thing, even though the list might be full, it's hard to resist a promising talent.

Though I list the size of their lists in my book, many agents may say they have fewer clients than they do – because that looks better. The same is true if you check clients and size of list on IMDbPro.

An agency with a lot of series regulars has clients who are out of circulation for a large part of the year and don't require much upkeep, which gives the agent time to attend to other clients. It's dicey. Bottom line is how much attention you find you are/are not getting.

It's easy to get lost on a large list. It's easy to get lost on a small list too. It all depends on if you can keep up their enthusiasm.

It's all very well to have stamina, discern talent, have a short list, and be a great salesman. I take that as a given. But there are two other attributes that separate the contenders from the also-rans.

Access and Stature

The dictionary defines the word access as "ability to approach" or "admittance." Since the conglomerate agencies have many stars on their lists, they have plenty of ability to approach. If the studios, networks, and producers do not return their phone calls, they might find the agency retaliating by withholding their important stars.

Stature on the other hand is different entirely. Webster defines the word as "level of achievement." Thus, Phil Adelman (BRS/Gage) and Bruce Ostler (Bret Adams) certainly have more stature than some beginning agent at WME, but because Adelman and Bruce don't have an equal number of bankable stars, they might not have as much access. Get both stature and access if you can, but if you have to choose, go with access.

The central issue is, how do you choose the agent who will provide the opportunity for you to be gainfully employed in the business?

Wrap Up

The Ideal Client
✓ has talent
✓ possesses contagious emotions
✓ displays a singular personality
✓ exhibits professionalism
✓ manifests self-knowledge
✓ shows drive
✓ is innately likeable
✓ maintains mental health
✓ is well-trained
✓ boasts a good resume

The Ideal Agent
✓ is aggressive
✓ has stature
✓ has access
✓ is enthusiastic
✓ shares the actor's career vision
✓ has optimum actor/rep ratio
✓ has integrity

chapter 9

Star/Conglomerate Agencies

I guess we've all heard the joke about the actor who killed four people, ran over a baby, bombed a building, ran across the street into CAA and was never seen again. It's the quintessential actor story about the wisdom of being signed by a conglomerate agency.

It does seem like it would be nice to have the same agent as Brad Pitt and Angelina Jolie, but is that really a good choice for you? The question is perplexing and research doesn't support a definitive answer. As in all other important decisions, who to marry, where to go to college, whether or not to have elective surgery, etc., your decision must be based upon a combination of investigation and instinct.

Research leads to the conclusion that star agencies (CAA, UTA, WME, ICM Partners, etc.) have more information and, *if they want to*, the best likelihood of getting you in for meetings, auditions, and ultimately jobs.

A successful writer friend of mine was repped by one of the large conglomerates. She was making about $300,000 a year and an employer owed her money. She kept calling her agent asking him to pursue it.

The agent was becoming increasingly irritated with her calls. She finally left when the agent said, "I really wish you were more successful and made more money so I wouldn't have to keep having these conversations with you."

If $300,000 a year is not enough to get the attention of the big guys, then there are a lot of agents who will take your calls and treat you respectfully for a lot less.

Casting Directors/Star Agencies

I asked one casting director, "Who do you call first and why?" He answered, "CAA, UTA, WME, ICM Partners," and also mentioned the name of a one-person office. The casting director said that although he can cast all the interesting parts from the conglomerates, he dare not skip this particular office because everyone on the list was special and capable of brilliance.

He explained that although many prestigious independent agents have hot new actors, the process is like shopping for a suit. If you want the best suit, you go to Bergdorf Goodman first. At Bloomingdale's you can get a beautiful suit and expect to spend a comparable amount of money, but Bergdorf has cachet, the perception that it is the source for the new and the unusual.

Casting directors also tell me they prefer dealing with distinguished independent agents like DGRW, BRS/Gage, Cornerstone Talent, Carlton, Goddard & Freer Talent and others and that an actor would be crazy to leave such caring families for a conglomerate.

But, since CAA, UTA, WME and ICM Partners have made it their business to represent all the creative elements of the business, casting executives and producers acknowledge that if they want to do business with star actors, writers, and directors, they will have to deal with the star agents and succumb to a certain amount of blackmail. "Take this one or you don't get that one," for example. So if they care, perhaps they could increase your employment possibilities.

It makes sense to choose an agency with a powerful client list, information, and stature. However, a well known actress friend has other thoughts. The actress works mostly in film, but had recently been doing more theatre, an activity not prized by star agencies since relatively little money is involved.

She ended up leaving the agency. "It's too much trouble to keep up with all those agents. They won't all come and see your work. Who needs it?"

Would she return to the conglomerate if she got hot? Her answer was illuminating: "I was hot when I was at the smaller agency. My name was on everybody's list. I didn't need to have a big office behind me. The only way I'd ever go back to a big agency is with a very strong manager. That way the manager could call and keep up with all those agents. So, no, I don't think it's necessarily a better business decision to be at a conglomerate."

It's true that the conglomerates have more power and information, but do those attributes compensate for lack of personal attention? The strength of the large agencies comes from having A-list stars. The bankable stars get the attention of the buyers and the agents.

Power Structure

When you have Brie Larson and Emma Stone on your list, you have the attention of the buyers. Of course, if you are Brie or Emma, you don't need star agencies because you are the power. If you are not Brie or Emma, you are filler.

A big star was in the final stages of closing a deal on a big new movie, when a higher-priced star at the same agency decided he was interested in the project. The original plans were shelved and the bigger paycheck did the movie.

An independent agent might do the same thing, but the chances are less likely that he will be representing you and your closest competitor.

Packaging

A large agency, one representing writers, directors, producers, and actors has a script written by one of its writers with a great part for one of its stars or first-billed actors. It then selects one of its directors and/or producers and calls ABC and says, "Our star writer has just written a terrific script for our star actress and our star director is interested. Are you?" ABC says, "Yes," and a package is sold.

Television pilots, TV movies and theatrical films are merchandised in this way. This phenomenon is called packaging. Non-star actors frequently choose agencies with package potential because they feel they too will get jobs out of the arrangement. The truth is that you can maybe package the first-billed actor and possibly the second actor, but at that point people at the studios and the networks want their creative input. If you are cast in a project your agency packages, your agent is not allowed to charge commission because he is already getting a fat packaging fee. This can be a good deal since you won't have to pay commission, but it offers no incentive for your agent to place you in the package.

He cares much more about the packaging fee and doesn't care much who is cast in it. And if you are tied up in a job for which the agent is not collecting commission, he is unable to sell you for something on which he can make money.

There are many horror stories recounting star clients who were never told of an offer because the agent was withholding the star's services in order to get a packaging fee for the project. If the producers didn't go for it, the actor or writer or director never knew there had been an offer.

The value of packaging lies more importantly in the amount of access your agent is able to have with the buyers. Because the agent or someone at his company is talking to the buyers daily, there's naturally more of a feeling of comradeship.

Money Money Money Money

The big agencies are about money. They have a big overhead. But actors have different needs. James Woods, interviewed by Stephen Rebello, spoke of a harrowing two years at CAA:

If there was anybody meant to star in a Tarantino movie, it's me. Ten days after I went with Toni Howard and Ed Limato at ICM, they sent me up to meet Tarantino. The first words out of his mouth were, "Finally, I get to meet James Woods".

I'm sitting there thinking, "I haven't worked on a decent movie in two years and he's saying this?" I said, "What do you mean?" and he said, "I wrote Mr. So-and-So in Reservoir Dogs *for you".*

I don't want to say the exact role because the actor who played the role is really wonderful. I said, "Look, I've had a real bad year, so could you explain why you didn't offer it to me if you wrote it for me?" He said, "We made a cash offer five times."

Of course, it was for less money than my [former] agents wanted me to work for, but that's not the point. I wanted to cry. I'd rather work for a third of my salary and make Reservoir Dogs. *But I didn't get to do* Reservoir Dogs, *didn't get to know Quentin, so I didn't get to do* True Romance *or* Pulp Fiction.

All because somebody else decided money was more important. They were treating me like I was an idiot. I made less money this year doing six movies than I made when I was at CAA doing two movies. And I couldn't be happier.
— Movieline[15]

The problem is that they're too big and they can't possibly function as effectively for an individual client as any number of not huge agencies. I don't see it, even for a star. I don't see the personal attention. To me, negotiation is easy. You keep saying no until you get what you want.
— Kenneth Kaplan, The Gersh Agency

Kenneth told me that when he was still an independent agent in New York. Since then, he has moved to The Gersh Agency, a bi-coastal agency with an important list of actors, writers, directors and below-the-line personnel. What does he say now?

Yeah. I know I said some things about conglomerate agencies in your last book. But I have to admit that being able to work from the script instead of the Breakdown, which is really somebody else's interpretation of what the script is, plus access to directors and producers, really does take a lot of frustration out of being an agent.
— Kenneth Kaplan, The Gersh Agency

There are many prestigious independent agencies that have had a shot at the big time and chose to go back to a more intimate way of doing business. One of my favorite agents has groomed several stars. When those actors became more successful and demanding, the agent grew tired of being awakened at midnight to endlessly discuss the next career move. It was disappointing when the actors went to WME or ICM Partners, but the agent just didn't see himself as a babysitter.

Gene Parseghian was still at WME when he confessed that there were days when he wished he still had a small office with three or four people and twenty clients, tops. Today, Gene is a manager with a much smaller client list.

Jack Nicholson's agent, Sandy Bresler, left William Morris and started his own office. When that got too big for him, he left and started his own smaller office again. Of course, he did take Nicholson with him. That helped.

Conglomerates are not equipped to handle actors who are not making a lot of money. They don't develop talent. They take you while you're hot and they drop you when you're not.

A friend was on a soap for ten years while her conglomerate agent collected 10%. When her character was written out, she went for an entire year without an audition at which point her agency dropped her.

You're Aging Even As You Read This

Star agencies are interested in youth, not just for the longevity factor, but because the most lucrative jobs in television and film (the leads) are for young, good-looking actors. So if you have the look and manage to snag a nice part in a film that makes some money, you may well have the option of being signed by one of the big star agencies.

If they are able to move your career forward quickly, you'll be well served. The conglomerates have access to not only the biggest star actors, but they also have the star writers and directors.

But if/when your career hits a snag and you have some downtime, as we've discussed before, the conglomerates have a very high overhead and they don't have time to nurture careers. They can move you forward while you have momentum. Once that's lost, you'll have to stoke it up again on your own.

A director friend declared that CAA was marvelous for him when he was hot with a new film, but when he let himself cool down by taking too long to make up his mind for his next project, the agents lost interest because there was nothing new to talk about. Once he came up with a project to sell, CAA was terrific at promoting it and helping him realize his goal. He took responsibility for his part in cooling down and hasn't let it happen again.

Part of being a grown up is understanding how the business works and taking responsibility for dropping the ball if you did and taking steps to get back in the game on your own.

For insights into the business in all areas, particularly into life at the star agencies, I recommend Mark Litwak's book, *Reel Power*. All of us may dream of the validation we might feel as a CAA client but as James Woods said in the Rebello interview, sometimes that validation costs more than we might like to pay:

All CAA thinks about is the biggest salary you can get, period. My [former] agents were saying stuff like, "If you star in a movie with so-and-so, and it makes $100 million, then you can work with anybody." I said, "You know what? I beg to differ. I don't think that if you do a movie with Pauly Shore, with all due respect, Sydney Pollack is then going to hire you."
— Movieline[16]

Who's Who of the Star Agencies?

If you check out Companies/Agencies at IMDbPro, you'll get a page that lists the agencies according to their Companymeter. Whether that number is based on power, clients, size, who knows? On this day in time, they list: CAA followed by WME, UTA, ICM Partners, The Gersh Ageny, Paradigm, London's Independent Talent Group , APA, Innovative and Troika (also in London).

Within the ranks of the big agencies, there is constant warfare and defection. In 2015, five CAA agents defected to UTA with their famous clients intact:

On the morning of March 31, Richard Lovett, newly arrived in Santa Fe, N.M., for a set visit, called his Creative Artists Agency partner Bryan Lourd, who was in New York dealing with a family illness. He had bad news: Five agents, whose clients include Chris Pratt, Will Ferrell and Melissa McCarthy, had just messengered their resignations and defected to United Talent Agency. None of them had informed Lovett or Lourd directly. "It was such a betrayal on a personal level," says one agency source.

That was the beginning of one of the most tempestuous weeks in both companies' histories, as UTA CEO Jeremy Zimmer jubilantly welcomed the new arrivals (whose numbers would climb to 11 agents within a week) during a companywide meeting, while CAA scrambled to keep clients and strategize how to fight back.
— The Hollywood Reporter[17]

The defections seemed to be tied to CAA's corporate climate:

Friends of the departing agents say they had been disgruntled for some time and that the defections are symptomatic of a widespread resentment among staffers at CAA; former agents and other ex-employees complain that the agency's top partners "cashed out" with the TPG deal and have not invested in growing the agency to the degree that rival WME has done.
— Ibid[18]

No agency has suffered the pitfalls of outside money as much as ICM, still rebuilding from the devastating consequences that flowed from selling to Rizvi Traverse in 2005. "It's a terrible idea to let private equity into your company," says a former ICM agent. "The horror of [Suhail] Rizvi was that he took all the receivables on day one." When the agency packaged two of the biggest hits in recent television history, Modern Family *and* The Big Bang Theory, *there was nothing to prevent him from draining away those profits, too. Devastating defections followed before a group of senior agents bought Rizvi out in 2012.*
— hollywoodreporter.com/news/personal-epic-inside-drama-behind-799740
— Ibid[19]

If you take the time to read about the agencies and their histories online and in the media, you'll notice that defections of agents and/or clients from agencies are nothing new.

What is new is the increasing number of big agencies that are no longer privately owned and live at the whim of their bottom-line-focused-money-men making life for the agents and stars now in business with non-showbusiness principals more uncertain.

I combined information about the star agency hierarchy from IMDbPro and a *Hollywood Reporter* article by Rebecca Sun that appeared in print on June 12, 2015. You can check out all Sun's data online at hollywoodreporter.com/news/thr-guide-7-major-hollywood-799743.

Agency for the Performing Arts (APA): APA has 3,400 clients and 210 agents and 15 managing partners. Founded in 1962 by former MCA agents David Baumgarten, Roger Vorce and Harvey Litwin, they have offices in Los Angeles, New York and Nashville. This privately owned comedy-strong company is led by President and CEO Jim Gosnell. Clients include: Gary Oldman, Gina Rodriguez, Uzo Aduba, Wesley Snipes, Louis C.K., Amy Schumer and Kevin Hart. Their Physical Production Department reps below-the-line talent.

Creative Artists Agency (CAA): CAA was founded in 1975 by defecting WMA agents Mike Rosenfeld, Michael Ovitz, Ron Meyer, Bill Haber and Rowland Perkins. They have 3220 clients and 259 agents. Listed by IMDbPro at #1, their majority shareholder is TPG Capital. The managing partners are Kevin Huvane, Steve Lafferty, Rob Light, Bryan Lourd, Richard Lovett (president), David O'Connor and Michael Rubel. One reason CAA is the biggest agency is the diversification. No longer just representing actors, writers, directors, composers, broadcasters and traditional showbiz infrastructure, CAA's acquisition of athletics giant IMG and Professional Bull Riders, expanded their reach even further. With departments of Basketball, Booking, Film Finance and Sales, Games, Music Sponsorship, Alternative, Sports

Endorsements, Motion Picture, Theatrical, Comedy Touring, Personal Appearances, Publicity, Books, Literary Talent, TV Literary, Motion Picture Literary and Commercial Endorsements, they pretty much have things covered. Clients include: Robert Downey, Jr., Jennifer Lawrence, Matthew McConaughey, Melissa McCarthy and Peyton Manning.

The Gersh Agency: The Gersh Agency was founded in 1949 by one of the last agents from Hollywood's golden age, Phil Gersh. His sons Bob and David, are now Co-Presidents and Leslie Siebert is senior managing partner. This privately owned company has about 2000 clients, 75 agents plus 16 partner agents, with offices in LA and NY.

Gersh's core business remains repping an impressive roster of steadily working actors whose faces might be more recognizable than their names. Still, 2015 Oscar winners Patricia Arquette and JK Simmons make for nice calling cards. Gersh also reps Adam Driver, Elizabeth Olson, Kristen Stewart and Taylor Schilling. In 2009, Gersh established a film financing/packaging division led by producer Jay Cohen. Marie Perry(Skouras Agency) heads a commercial production division that reps below-the-line talent for ads and music videos.

ICM Partners: ICM Partners was formed with the 1975 merger of Creative Management Associates and International Famous Agency.

ICM Partners has 125 agents. In addition to their glittering actor clients, TV writer-producers Shonda Rhimes and Vince Gilligan are but two of ICMP's powerful literary stars. ICMP's important publishing division reps 100 NY Times best-sellers each year. Their strong concert division has Beyoncé, Celine Dion and Jerry Seinfeld leading the pack.

Paradigm: Paradigm was founded in 1992 by Sam Gores through mergers and acquisitions of several boutiques. There are 2500 clients and 160 agents. They have offices in Los Angeles, New York, and important music satellites in Nashville and Monterey, CA. Privately owned, Gores is Chairman and CEO while Debbee Klein, Andrew Ruf,

Rand Holston and Adam Kanter are listed as talent and lit leaders. Chip Hooper and Marty Diamond lead the large music contingent. Clients include: Shailene Woodley, Mark Harmon, Ava DuVernay, Stephen King, Craig Bierko, Ed O'Neil.

UTA: UTA was formed when important literary office Bauer-Benedek merged with Leading Artists in 1991. Privately owned, UTA sports 3000 + clients. They have 200 agents and 46 agent partners with offices in Los Angeles and New York. Managing directors David Kramer, Jay Sures and Jeremy Zimmer (CEO); chairman Jim Berkus; co-founder Peter Benedek; Tracey Jacobs and Matt Rice; special adviser Jason Heyman. The April defection of CAA comedy agents to UTA with clients Chris Platt, Will Ferrell, Zach Galifianakis, etc. in tow make UTA increasingly powerful. Supposedly UTA's corporate climate is more humanistic than CAA, so who knows who will be coming next? UTA is also the top broadcast news agency since acquiring NS Bienstock in 2014. UTA recently launched a fine arts division. UTA's Production Department was started in 1994 and represents Producers, Directors of Photography, Production Designers, Costume Designers, Editors, Visual Effects Supervisors, First Assistant Directors, Second Unit Directors and Stunt Coordinators. Other clients: Channing Tatum, Johnny Depp, Elizabeth Banks, Amy Schumer.

WME/IMG: WME is the result of Endeavor's 2009 takeover of the historic William Morris Agency and the 2014 acquisition of global sports and media giant IMG, quadrupling the agency's size and scope. WME/IMG has offices in Beverly Hills, London, Miami Beach, Nashville and New York. Private equity firm Silver Lake Partners holds 51% equity and wields the power here. Co-CEOs Ari Emanuel and Patrick Whitesell. Clients include: Mark Wahlberg, Jake Gyllenhaal, Jon Stewart, Stephen Colbert, Ben Affleck, Tina Fey, Christian Bale.

Is Bigger Better?

You could have a big agency with lots of information at its fingertips that isn't motivated to use it for you, or you might have a resourceful agent with his own office who is so enthusiastic about you that he uncovers just the information needed to get you a great part.

The big agencies come with scripts, limos, candy and flowers and the Full Court Press. When all is said and done, limos notwithstanding, you're going to have to make your decision based on what is important to you. Do you want a family member or do you want a corporation?

Wrap Up

Conglomerates
- ✓ have more information
- ✓ command more power
- ✓ offer more perks
- ✓ package
- ✓ may give less personal attention
- ✓ may provide less support in times of duress
- ✓ their advice is corporate
- ✓ will drop you when you cool

Distinguished Smaller Agencies Offer
- ✓ more love
- ✓ more personal attention
- ✓ more empathy
- ✓ more freedom to experiment
- ✓ might be more motivated
- ✓ have room for career fluctuations
- ✓ no limos
- ✓ no flowers
- ✓ no candy

chapter 10

Research & Follow-through

Unfortunately, agents do not send out resumes in search of clients. Even if they are looking for clients (and they are all looking for the client who will make them wealthy and powerful beyond their dreams), agents don't send out a list of their training, accomplishments, and/or a personality profile.

Beyond their list of clients now listed at IMDbPro, there is no obvious key to their worth. Therefore, it is up to you to conduct an investigation of your possible business partners.

You have taken your first step: you bought this book. I've already done a lot of research for you by interviewing agents, asking about their background, looking at their client lists, interviewing some of their clients, and in general engaging in conversations with anyone and everyone in the business who might have something informed to say about theatrical agents. I've also read everything that I could get my hands on regarding their journeys and the way the business is conducted.

You should begin to have agent conversations with everyone you know. If you are just beginning in the business and your contacts are limited to your peers, they will probably be just as uninformed as you. Never mind, ask anyway. You never know where information lurks.

Ask what they have done thus far to attract an agent. Ask if they have a wishlist of agents they would like to have. Ask if they were able to get an agent to talk to them and why they picked that agent.

If you are in a group of actors and someone is further along than you and has an agent, ask that actor for advice. Tell them that you don't want to be a pest, but because you are just starting you want to educate yourself about agents and could he fill you in. Ask if he met with several agents first and what that was like, and if so, how he made his decision.

Find out how he approached the agent for the meeting, and how he knew to call that agent. It's okay to ask every dumb question you can think of, but first announce that you want advice, not help, that you are there to learn. Try not to salivate. Don't totally monopolize the person. Ask your questions, be grateful and move on.

How to Score

You can't make an informed decision about your readiness to attract an agent or what kind of agent you seek until you educate yourself. Learn how the business really works, what you have a right to expect from an agent, what you can realistically expect of an agent, and what your contribution is to the mix.

Prepare yourself as an artist and as a business person so that you can operate on the level to which you aspire. If your work and presentation are careless, what kind of agent is going to want you?

Before he agrees to meet with you, an agent has done his homework. He's researched you. If you had prior representation, he's asked about it. If you've done any work, he's called casting directors who cast you to find out what you're like.

He's going to expect that you've done the same. It's more difficult for you, but it's not impossible.

Get On With It/Agent Research

After you've digested this book completely, go back and read the agency listings again and take notes. You'll learn the agent's lineage, education, clients, the size of his list, and have some idea of his style. If there is someone who interests you, check the index to see if the agent is quoted elsewhere in the book. Those quotations can give you additional clues about how the agent conducts business, views the world and how comfortable you might feel with him.

If you checked the agent's client list and don't recognize any of the names, that may just mean his clients are respected working actors whose names you don't happen to know or they could be up-and-coming actors who have not yet worked. You can only evaluate the agent accurately if you know exactly what his list means. If he only works freelance, that tells you something too.

If the only clients the agent has on his list are stars and you are just beginning, that agent is too far along for you. If the agent has bright-looking actors with no important credits, he is building his list. If you fit that client category, perhaps you and the agent can build credibility together. It's worth a shot.

If you are an actor of stature, you will be looking for an agent that lists some of your peers. There are always new young agencies that have opened in the last two or three years whose names may not be as well-known as older agencies, but who have real credibility. Usually the agents worked at larger offices, learned the business, groomed some clients and left the nest (frequently with some of the agency's choicest clients) to open their own agencies.

A subscription to IMDbPro costs only $12.95 per month and gives you lists of agencies, clients and their staff. You can get a free two week trial to see if it works for you. The information available paints a picture if you take the time to investigate. Search the agency and the agent that interests you. Check out the clients of the agency, how many they are, how many agents there are. How many clients does the agent you are interested in actually represent.

Click on some of the client names, particularly those you never heard of. See the last time they worked. You might have never heard of them, but they might still have impressive IMDb credits.

Read carefully though, I saw some actors with many credits, but on closer examination, those credits were shorts, possibly self produced. That doesn't denigrate the actor, but since it's self produced work, those credits don't reflect the agent.

As your research continues, you'll have fantasies about the large conglomerate agencies, but remember what we said in the previous chapter, there are many pros and cons to representation by star agencies at every level of one's career.

While you are salivating about life at William Morris Endeavor, consider that most stars come to celebrity agencies after they've achieved a level of stature and access that financially justified the interest of the conglomerate agency.

Remember, WME, CAA, UTA and ICM Partners do not offer career-building services. Although star representation enhances some careers, it is not true in all cases. In making your agent selections, make sure you are seeking an agent you have the credits to attract: George Clooney's agent is probably not going to be interested.

Make sure clients on the agent's list are your peers. It's all very well and good to think big, but you must walk before you run. Don't expect an agent who has spent years building his credibility to be interested in someone who just got off the bus. You must effectively agent yourself until you are at a point that a credible agent will give you a hearing.

I met a young actor with no credentials who arrived in California and managed to hustle a meeting with an agent far above him in stature. This was before we all had samples of our work on our computers and the agents wanted to see some film. Although he had none, the actor said his film was in New York and that he would send for it. He volunteered to do a scene in the agent's office and ended up getting signed – then he confessed there was no film.

A year and no jobs later the actor angrily left the agent in search of another, saying the agent didn't work for him. It didn't occur to the actor that the reason he had no jobs was because he was not ready for representation on that level. Not only that, once having landed the agent, the actor totally lost all the hustle that undoubtedly appealed to the agent. Instead of learning from the experience and rethinking his approach, he did what many actors do: he blamed the agent.

When you're in pain, it's tempting to lash out at whoever is closest, but the common element in all our problems is ourselves. The day I figured that out, I was depressed until I figured out the plus side: if my problems were caused by others, I was powerless, but if the problem was me? Hey, I can change me.

I feel sorry for the people who spend all their time trying to use various forms of manipulation to get an agent while their contemporaries are working and learning. And the ones working at working will rise right up. The people who were assuming it's some kind of game will disappear.
— Fifi Oscard

Who Do You Love?

At this point, you should have some idea of which agents appeal to you. Some names will keep coming up. Make a list. Even if you know you are only interested in Jim Wilheim or Mark Redanty, target at least five names. You can't intelligently make a choice unless you have something to compare. You don't know that you like Agent A best unless you have seen Agent B and Agent C.

It's time to ask advice from casting directors with whom you have formed relationships. A CD who has hired you will probably be pleased that you asked his opinion. Tell him you are agent shopping and that you would like to run a few names by him. Also ask for any names he might like to add to your list. Listen to the casting director's opinion, but remember that he has a far different relationship with an agent than you will have. Make your own decision.

At this point your research is based on style, stature, access, size of list, word of mouth, and fantasy. Let's forge ahead to face-to-face encounters.

Getting a Meeting

The best way to contact anyone is through a referral. If you know someone on the agent's list who will act as a go-between, this is good. If a casting director whose advice you have sought offers to call, this is better, but don't put the CD on the spot by asking her to recommend you. If you ask for advice about agents and she feels comfortable recommending you, she will. If she doesn't, be thankful for the advice.

If someone you contact just says, "use my name," that is a polite brush-off. Unless a call is made, the referral is useless. Anyone can call and say, "Francine Maisler told me to call." Unless Francine picks up the phone for you, it doesn't count. If you are creative and have been doing your homework, you will be able to find someone who knows someone.

Winning an Oscar, a Tony or an Emmy gets people on the phone. In the past I told the Young and Beautiful to drop a picture off looking as Y&B as possible. These days for security reasons most doors are locked and won't even crack an inch to receive a picture.

If you want to give it a shot and a door is opened to you, it can be a short-cut. It is sad for the rest of us, but true, if you are really Y&B and can speak at all, few will require that you do much more. Cash in on it.

Since Y&B doesn't linger long, if you are smart, you will study while cashing. You may want to work in those gray years of your thirties and beyond.

You're not Y&B? Me neither. If you are just starting in the business or don't have any strong credits, concentrate on classes. Join theatre groups. Get involved with showcases. View as much theatre, film and television as possible. Go backstage and congratulate the actors afterwards even if you don't know them. If the writer and/or director is there and you liked the work, say so and give them your card and tell them you want to see the next thing they do and if they ever need help with ANYthing to give you a call. If you can find their email address, write the next day and invite them to tea. This is not about getting a job, it's about building a place in the theatre fraternity.

Begin making a list of actors/writers/directors with whom you would like to work. Align yourself with peers whose work you respect. Form a group that includes all of the above and focus on furthering each other's careers by working together.

If all you do is get together in someone's living room once a week and read a writer's new work or a current or classic play, you have accomplished a lot. Write your own independent movie. I used the Kodak Z18 several years ago to shoot the little film now on youtube (just type in K Callan). The camera only cost about $200 (they're probably cheaper now) and shoots in high resolution. The Duplas Brothers produced the 2015 feature release *Tangerine* which was shot entirely on an iPhone for $100,000. Where there is a will, there is a way.

Take a writing and/or directing seminar. You need to expand your horizons into those fields anyway. Make yourself available to read scripts or work in independent films. New York is the capital of the independent film movement.

Check out the film school at NYU and leave a picture and resume. Read the bulletin board. Volunteer to do anything that needs doing and you will gain access to the Spielbergs of tomorrow. Independent Feature Project (IFP) is also a good connection.

Don't approach actors or casting directors asking for meetings until you build up your resume and have something to show them. I spoke to an agent who told me that several young agent-shopping actors banded together and sent her a basket of goodies along with their 8x10s and resumes.

This definitely got the agent's attention. The downside was that the actors were still just too green to be looking for an agent. Don't blow your chances by getting people to look at you before you are ready.

I've always spoken ill of casting director workshops since I think that most actors expect to be cast from these sessions. Even though the big signs say, "you will not get cast from this, the session is informational," the actor pays his money and crosses his fingers. I still tend to think CD workshops don't really pay off in jobs, but an agent I interviewed said he had a call from a CD who had seen three of his clients in a workshop and asked to meet them all. So, clearly I don't know anything about this. If you are new and marketable, then obviously it is a good idea.

If you are packaged and you are ready and you get a credible casting director (not some assistant there to pick up $100 without any real power to cast) you could be cast.

It's a crap shoot, but it's worth trying. Somebody wins in craps.

Once You Are Ready

If you have graduated from a connected school and/or have some decent credits and/or an electronic sample of your work and have a clear idea how you should be marketed, it's time to begin. Send a letter or e-mail to a specific agent, not just the name of the agency. Check the agency preference for electronic or snail mail submissions. If you are sending via snail mail, the picture and resume should follow two days later. A cover letter accompanies material. Single letters get read; pictures and resumes tend to sit on the "whenever I get to it" stack.

Make sure your letter is written on good stationery. The feel of expensive paper makes an unconscious impression that the writer is to be taken seriously. Say who you are and why you are writing. State that you are interested in representation, that you are impressed with the agent's client list (mention somebody's name), and that your credits compare favorably. Mention any impressive credits.

I've provided an example below to stimulate your thinking.

Dear Mary Smith:

I've just moved to New York from Timbuktu and am interested in representation. I met George Brown and Sheila Jones in Karen Ludwig's acting class. They told me they have worked through you.

Since I am in their peer group, I thought I might fit in with your client list. Although I am new to town, I do have a few credits. I met John Casting Director and have worked two jobs through him: *Hello Everyone* and *It Pays to Study*.

The parts were small, but it was repeat business and everyone has to start somewhere. I'm compiling an audition tape. My picture and resume will be in your office by Thursday. I'll call on Friday to see if you have a few minutes and might be interested in meeting me. In the meantime, my reel and my picture and resume are online at hopefulactor.com. I'm looking forward to meeting you.

Sincerely,
Hopeful Actor

When you write to an agent, remember that on Mondays, there is a barrage of mail, so your picture might garner more interest arriving mid-week.

Make sure your picture and resume tell the truth and arrive when you promised them. If your letter has stirred interest, your picture will be opened immediately. Call the day after your picture arrives.

When you call (late afternoon is best), be dynamic and be brief. Be a person the agent wants to talk to. If he doesn't want a meeting, get over the disappointment and get on to the next agent on your list. Try to set up meetings with at least three agents and plan all the details of the meeting.

Be on time and look terrific. This is a job interview, after all. Choose clothing that makes you feel good and look successful and that suggests you take pride in yourself. Bright colors not only make people remember you, but they usually make you feel good too. Remember, in today's world packaging is at least as important as product.

Go in and be yourself. Be natural and forthright. Don't bad-mouth other agents. If you are leaving another agent, don't get into details. If the agent asks, just say it wasn't working out. Agents are all members of the same fraternity. Unless this agent is stealing you from someone else, he will be at least a little anxious about why you are leaving. If you bad-mouth another agent, the agent will wonder, subconsciously at least, what you will say about him. Not only that, it's not good for you to be indulging in negative energy.

In general, don't talk too much. Give yourself a chance to get comfortable. Adjust to the environment. Notice the surroundings. Comment on them. Talk about the weather. Talk about the stock market, the basketball game or the last play you saw. That's a great topic. It gives you each a chance to check out the other's taste. Don't just agree with him. Say what you think. If you hated it, say it just didn't work for you.

This is a first date. You are both trying to figure out if you want one another. If you've seen one of his clients in something and liked it, say so. Don't be afraid to ask questions, but use common sense. It's not what you say, it's how you say it.

Phrase questions in a positive vein. Discuss casting directors that you know and have worked for. Ask which CDs the office has ties with. Tell the agent your plans. Mention the kind of roles that you feel you are ready for and that you feel you have the credits to support. Ask his opinion. Are you on the same wavelength? Don't just send out; make sure you are also receiving.

Find out how the office works. If you are being interviewed by the owner and there are other agents, ask the owner if he will be representing you personally. Many owners are not involved in agenting on a day-to-day basis.

Check office policy about phone calls. Are you welcome to call? Does the agent want feedback after each audition? What's the protocol for dropping by? Will he consistently view your work? Will he consult with you before turning down work? Explore your feelings about these issues before the meeting.

If you need to speak to your agent on a regular basis, now's the time to say so. Does the office have a policy of regularly requesting audition material for their actors at least a day in advance of the audition? Let him know what you require to be at your best. If these conversations turn the agent off, better to find out now. This is the time to assess the chemistry between the two of you.

Make a mental note right now that you will read this chapter over again right before you go to meet an agent.

What makes a good agent? Partially the chemistry between an actor and the agent and partially the chemistry that goes on between the agent and the casting director; that they can communicate on an intelligent, non-whining wavelength. A good agent has to be able to not be so restricted by casting information and the Breakdown, so boxed in by what they read that they don't expand the possibilities. And finally, that they can get people appointments for good work.
– Marvin Starkman, producer

During the meetings, be alert. Intangible signs reveal a person. Note how he treats his employees, if he really listens, body language, how he is on the phone. How do you feel when he's speaking to you? What's the subtext? The agent will want to know the CDs with whom you have relationships. Review this information so you can converse easily and intelligently. Even if your specialty is playing dumb blondes, your agent will feel more comfortable about making a commitment to a person who is going to be an informed business partner.

Morgan Fairchild came in, and out of the hundreds and hundreds of actresses and actors that I have seen and had appointments with, I've never been literally interviewed by an actress: "Okay, what have you done? Where are you going?" Incredible. She interviewed me. Yes, I was turned off to a degree, but I was so impressed by her brilliant mind and her smarts that I thought to myself, "Gal, even without me, you're going to go very far." She came in here and she knew where she was going and she interviewed me and I thought, "That's fantastic."
– Beverly Anderson

Beverly points out an important truth. Although she was turned off by Fairchild's approach, she saw the potential. If you want an agent to want you, it's like any other relationship, you can't be desperate. It's important to be respectful, but don't genuflect.

Tips for Meetings

1. If you haven't been hitting the gym, you've got a few months to shape up. Do it! In the short period of time you've got to perform, a physical impression will be as strong as any other you can make. Agents want their new clients to be appropriate for the roles that are out there, which are almost uniformly leading roles.

2. Unless you are another Kenneth Branagh, Shakespearean scenes are usually not as appropriate or as effective for an audience as

contemporary material. Avoid Moliere, Chekhov and other classics like the plague. Outside the context of the plays these scenes come off as dull.

3. Shorter is better in regard to scenes. Most people make up their minds about you in the first twenty or thirty seconds. Don't drag it out. No scene should be longer than two or three minutes.

4. Funny is better than anything, if you can handle comedy. Agents sit through a lot of scenes, laughter makes them grateful.

5. Try to avoid scenes that are done every year. The "Are You a Homosexual" scene from *Angels in America* is so overdone. There are other scenes in that play.

6. If you're going to do a scene from a film (which is fine) try to avoid scenes with are linked inextricably to certain performances.

7. Doing John Travolta or Samuel L. Jackson from *Pulp Fiction,* or Brando from *On the Waterfront* is bad. Most actors aren't going to be able to compete with our memories of the original.

8. Dress simply but to flatter. Guys should wear jeans or slacks and t-shirts to show off their physique. Women should wear skirts or dresses and heels to do the same.

9. A showcase is NOT the time to explore your ethnic, racial, sexual or gender identity.

10. Don't do material just to shock or to talk about the inner you. More often than not it comes off as amateurish and polemic.

11. Finally, remember why you're there. It's not about art. It's about getting people to like you, to hire you, to sign you.

And a special tip from Jim Wilhelm at DGRW:

Make us feel something. Good acting has the power to make us laugh or make us cry. In two or three minutes, those are the buttons to push.
– Jim Wilhelm/DGRW

Closing the Meeting

Now that you have met the agent, focused on his accomplishments, office and personnel, impressed him with your straightforwardness, drive, punctuality, resume, appearance, and grasp of the business and your place within it, underscore that by knowing when it's time to leave. Sooner is better than later.

Make it clear that you are having such a good time you could stay all day, but you realize that he is busy and that you just have time to make your voice lesson. It doesn't matter where you are going. Just have a real appointment to go to and leave.

Suggest that you both think about the meeting for a day or two and set a definite time for when you will get back to him or vice-versa. If he asks if you are meeting other agents, be truthful.

If he's last on your list, mention that you need to go home and digest all the information. He will probably have to have a meeting with his staff before making a decision. Let him know you were pleased with the meeting. Even if it was not your finest moment or his, be gracious. After all, you both did your best.

My advice is to hurry home and write down all your feelings about the meeting and put them away for twenty-four hours. Then write your feelings down again and compare them. When I was interviewing agents for this book, I found I would have signed with almost any of them on the spot. They are all salesmen and they were all charming.

The next day I had more perspective. The excitement of the

meeting had worn off and I was able to discern reality more clearly.

If the agent said he would get in touch with you and he doesn't, leave it. There are others on your list. If he forgot you, do you want him as your agent? If he is rejecting you, don't insist he do it to your face. Remember, you are choosing an agent. The traits you look for in a pal are not necessarily the qualities you desire in an agent.

If you want an agent on a higher level who's not interested, don't be deterred. There are other agents on that level. If they all turn you down, then perhaps you are not as far along as you think. This just means you need to do more work on yourself until you are ready for those agents. If you feel you really must have representation at this time, you may need to pursue an agent on a lower level. But let's think positive.

Just like any other relationship, you're going to click with some and not with others. The agent is looking to see if there is a connection, if there isn't, there is a better agent for you and client for him.

When you have a meeting with an agent, make sure you touch base with everyone afterward. Send a thank you note or a card and, if you do decide to go with another agent, let them know how much you enjoyed meeting him and that you are appreciative of his time.

Even if they say, "if you don't go with us, you don't need to call back," make the effort. If you treat people politely, you'll find that's the way people treat you.
– Gary Krasny, The Krasny Office, Inc.

Making the Decision
The late Mike Nichols gave a speech to his actors one opening night:

Just go out there and have a good time. Don't let it worry you that the New York Times is out there, that every important media person in the world is watching you, that we've worked for days and weeks and months on this production, that the investors are going to lose their houses if it doesn't go well, that the writer will commit suicide and that it will be the end of your careers if you make one misstep. Just go out there and have a good time.

I think that's the way many of us feel about choosing an agent. At the beginning of my career, I freelanced much longer than was career-appropriate because I was afraid of making a wrong decision that I was just sure could have irrevocable consequences on my career.

I find that actors are sometimes overly cautious. They are sometimes guided by anxiety or fear and that leads one to say, "No, I'm going to wait," when there is nothing to lose by signing with a particular agent who is interested.

If it doesn't work, the actor can always get out of it. It's only for a year. There is so much more that can be done when there is an effective responsible agent at work that sometimes it's an actor's insecurity that holds him back, and I think wrongly so.
– Gene Parseghian, Manager Parseghian Planco

There are some agents who don't share Gene's POV. Many would rather not sign you if they feel you are not ready for a long-term commitment. If you're in a position where you trust yourself and your instincts as an actor, then trust yourself to make a good decision. Innovative's Alan Willig put it very well: *Know thyself and trust your agent.*

Wrap Up
Research
- ✓ peruse this book
- ✓ consult casting directors
- ✓ IMDbPro
- ✓ don't underestimate word of mouth
- ✓ have face-to-face meetings

Tools to Set Up Meetings
- ✓ referrals
- ✓ good credits
- ✓ awards
- ✓ beauty
- ✓ audition DVDs/electronic sample of your work

✓ a well-written note stating your credits
✓ picture and credible resume

The Meeting
✓ be punctual
✓ act intelligently
✓ be well-dressed
✓ be focused
✓ know what you want
✓ ask for what you want
✓ entertain/engage/move the agents with good material
✓ read this chapter right before you go, it will focus you

After the Meeting
✓ don't overstay your welcome, end the meeting
✓ set definite time for follow-up
✓ send a nice note

chapter 11

The Partnership

Once you have made a decision to sign with an agent, there are many things to do. The next stop is your new partner's office to sign contracts and meet and start to learn about all the auxiliary people who will be working for you. Make notes as soon as you leave the office as to who is who and where they sit. Until you become more familiar with them, you can consult the map before each subsequent visit.

Leave a supply of pictures, resumes and DVDs. Be spare. Bringing more is always a good excuse for dropping by. Also leave a list for each agent of casting directors, producers and directors with whom you have relationships. Alphabetize them if you ever want them used. Also leave lists of your quotes (how much you were paid for your last jobs in theatre, film and television) plus information about billing. The more background you give your agent, the better he can represent you.

Now the real work begins. Remember the agent only gets 10% of the money. You can't really expect him to do 100% of the work.

How Do We Really Get Work?

How many of us have resented our agents when we have been requested for a job and all the agent had to do was negotiate? In fact, if all our jobs were requests, would we just have a lawyer negotiate and do away with the agent altogether? Or is the support and feedback worth something? And as Lynn Moore Oliver said in Chapter One, what about all the times he sent our pictures and/or talked about us when he wasn't able to get an appointment, so we never knew about it? Or all the appointments we went on and didn't get the job? That costs him time and money that we frequently don't consider when we're whining about his shortcomings.

Maybe our whole thought process about agents is incorrect. In our hearts, we really think the agent is going to get us a job. Based upon my years in the business and my research, I finally know that the agent does not get me work, he gets me opportunities. I get my own work. By my work. Not only by my ability to function well as an actress, but also by my ability (or not) to be who I am.

The times I have not worked as steadily have been directly connected to my rise and fall as a person. I went into a terrible depression when my children left home. I willed myself to be up, but it was just a loss that I had to mourn, and while I was mourning, I was not particularly attractive to casting directors or anybody else. You can change agents or mates or clothes sizes to try to make yourself feel better, but none of those things will change the fact that we all have to experience our lives in order to move through them.

These changes are reflected in our work and enrich us as performers. If one can remember to commit to experiencing the process instead of fighting it, the pain dissipates much faster.

So, although we can hope that agents are going to initiate work for us and introduce us to the casting directors, producers, directors, etc., what they are really going to do (over the span of a career) is negotiate for us, initiate meetings, arrange appointments when we are requested, and, hopefully, be supportive in our dark moments and help us retain our perspective in our bright moments. Notice I say moments. Neither state will last as long as it seems.

90 percent/10 percent

Although I've always been business oriented about my career, I never really thought about the ramifications of 90%-10% until I began doing the research for my books. When I finally signed with an agent in New York after successfully freelancing for a long time, I really did think that my hustling was over. Knowing what I know now, I realize all the ways I might have contributed to my career if I had agented more myself or at the very least paid closer attention. That's still hard to remember.

I own 10% of the business. I don't work for the actor. I'm on the board of directors

with him. My function is to maintain the stock and bring it up. That's the way I look at the function. I am there to maximize the positive and minimize the negative. Advise. Help. Guide.
– Scott Manners, Stone Manners Sainers Agency

If you're not working because you are in your mid-life crisis, divorce, whatever, you may not be able to readily fix it, but it's up to you to assume you have a problem and set out to fix it.
– Martin Gage, BRS/Gage Talent Agency

Because we are getting 90% of the money, we have to give up being cranky when we have to do 90% of the work. I assume you are willing to do that, if you only knew what that meant.

What the Actor Can Do

The actor's job is to give me something I can sell: a showcase, a new picture, a wonderful credit with a tour de force role. He has to be president of his own company, to treat the agent as his employee, to motivate him, to help guide him and to find a way to communicate with him so they can work as a team.
– Nancy Curtis, Harden Curtis Associates

Trust me to have your interests at heart. Check you messages frequently. Live your life but let me know before you buy a ticket out of town. Keep up with what's happening. Always be as prepared as possible for your auditions.
– Dianne Busch, Leading Artists, Inc.

Stay positive and make sure you look good, be part of the artistic community where information is passed around, and don't alienate your fellow artists.
– Diana Doussant, Leading Artists, Inc.

I like our clients to be pro-active and to stay in contact with the office. Let me know if you have a special relationship with a director who's casting his new production. Information is a powerful tool. Keep your resumes updated. Return calls promptly.

This is a partnership: both actor and agent working in tandem to build a career.
– Jeanne Nicolosi, Nicolosi & Co., Inc.

Develop some "radar" about the room, what they're open to across the table; it changes room-to-room and even hour-to-hour in the same room. Also, figure out how to act for "tape."
– Jay Kane, Talentworks New York

Nancy Curtis envisions her advice to all clients written on her tombstone: *Run your own company.* Her partner Mary Harden feels communication and a strong career plan are key to a successful actor-agent relationship.

Being an actor is an extraordinarily difficult job. You must be working on your craft and your person all the time, staying abreast of what's going on and keeping your instrument tuned.

The actor has to be clear about what he wants and what he says. If he says he doesn't want to go out of town, but then misses out on an important project because it was out of town and gets mad at his agent, the agent is going to say, "Well, you said you didn't want to go out of town." Once you put qualifiers on your career, you are not going to have as many auditions.
– Ellie Goldberg, Kerin-Goldberg Associates

It's very important for actors to network. If they have occasion to meet someone, follow up, stay in touch. It's important to keep your name afloat. I encourage proactivity, classes, showcases, open calls, trying to rustle up your own work.
– Jim Wilhelm, DGRW

You have to do a lot of work on your own. You sit around in circles with actors and everyone is saying, "well my agent didn't get me in on..." Now that I'm sitting in this chair, I can see that even the agent's best efforts sometimes go unnoticed.
You need the combination of the actors doing their work and trying to get themselves in. I tell actors, "If you know the musical director or the company

manager, go to them. You may get in that way easier than I can get you in." Getting an agent is not the be all, end all of the way to get work.
– Laurie Walton

Keep active. Even a lousy scene class will help you put less pressure on auditions.
– Jay Kane, Talentworks New York

Keep your acting wheel greased by doing readings. This is very valuable. Everyone does them. You get to know a group of people.
– Charles Kerin, Kerin-Goldberg Associates

Make sure that we have enough pictures and up-to-date resumes without our having to call. If you are a musical comedy performer, be willing to go to an open call if we have discussed this is what you should do. It's important to keep working whether it's in a class or a workshop or a group. Networking is important, but don't expect that every time your friend gets an appointment that you will too, and just because you call or drop in all the time, that we are necessarily going to think of you more. You don't want to become a pest. It is a business, in spite of how casual it is.
– Gary Krasny, The Krasny Office

You're not going to get every part you go in for. You're not going to get nearly every part you go in for. But what I never want to hear is, "He was late." "It was a slovenly audition." I don't even mind hearing, "She didn't do well." What I don't ever want to hear is, "He didn't pick up the sides." "She was ten minutes late."

All those things eventually hurt. Be prepared. If I'm putting my reputation on the line to get you the appointment, then put your reputation on the line enough so that I'm not looking like a fool for sending you in on it.
– Alan Willig, Don Buchwald & Associates

Alan puts it in perspective. In every audition, the agent puts his reputation on the line by sending you in and you put your reputation on the line by the quality of your work.

If you are unavailable for any reason (sick, vacation, working, whatever) please book out with us as soon as you know so we don't waste the casting directors' or our time working on jobs that you are not available to work. One of the worst things you can do as an actor is not show up for an audition. It makes you look extremely unprofessional and it reflects very poorly on us as a Management Company. So if you cannot make an audition for any reason, please be sure to let the your agent know immediately, or the CD know if the project is through LA Casting or Actors Access BEFORE the scheduled time of your audition. No shows will not be tolerated.

– Wendy Alane, WAW Entertainment Los Angeles

Always

✓ Have a pen and paper in hand when you return your agent's call.

✓ Check in often, return calls promptly.

✓ Take picture and resume to audition.

✓ Make sure your agent never gets a busy signal.

✓ Keep lines of communication open.

✓ Trust your agent and follow his advice from picture and resume to what kinds of shows to audition for.

✓ Make sure your picture is online at IMDb.com

✓ Keep pictures, resumes and reel up-to-date and available.

✓ Read the script before the audition.

✓ Arrive on time and well-prepared for the audition.

✓ Don't try to date the receptionist.

✓ Keep online casting website information current.

Clients and would be clients all want your agent's attention. What would be the best way to get your attention under the circumstances?

If I have to take time from my day to talk to you to see how your day is going, then I'm not on the phone doing what I am supposed to be doing. If you hear of a project, make a two-minute call, "I heard about this, is there anything in it for me?" That's the way to be a good partner.

– Ellie Goldberg, Kerin-Goldberg Associates

Actors need to understand that until 11:00 or 11:15 in the mornings, agents need to organize for the day, set up what Breakdowns they have to do, solve all the problems and handle the calls that came in at the end of the day before. This is organizational time for agents.

If the actor can just wait until 11:00 or 11:15 to call to find out about their next important piece of news, they would receive a more favorable response from the agent. Anytime after 11:15 and before 4:30 or 5:00.
– Gary Krasny, The Krasny Office

Networking

I know that networking is a dirty word to many of you. You say, "oh, I'm not good at all that," or, "I don't want to get a job just because I know someone," or "I'm here for art, not for commercialism," or some other elevated actor-jargon we all use from time to time to keep ourselves from testing our limits.

The most effective networking is done with your peers. You're not going to be able to pal around with Stephen Daldry or Joe Mantello. But you can pal around with the next Stephen Daldry and the next Joe Mantello by becoming involved with playwriting groups.

If you make it your business to attend theatre wherever it's happening, you will begin to notice who the writers and directors are who are starting their careers. Focus on those whose work appeals to you. Let them know you like their work. Give them your card and ask to be on their mailing list, take them to tea.

After you've seen their work a time or two, let them know that you are available if they need anything. Become involved in their projects. You will all develop together. It's hard to break into what seems like the charmed circle because people would rather work with people they already know and trust, particularly when a great deal of money is at stake. But you can see their point, wouldn't you rather work with friends and proven talent?

It is difficult behaving naturally around those who are higher on the food chain than you. But if you are well-read and cultivate an eye and ear for what's good, you'll soon contribute to the conversation and move up the food chain toward your goals, one rung at a time.

Don't You Really Want to Work?

I'm a pretty quick study and, with concentration, I have the ability to memorize audition material and not hold the script for something as brief as a commercial. When I was a beginning actor, however, I would always hold the pages because my background had taught me to be self-effacing. It seemed to me that putting the sides down was too pushy. It would make them think I really wanted the job.

On the day I decided to stop holding the script and take responsibility for the fact that I really did want the part, I began booking jobs.

I looked up self-effacing in the dictionary: it means self-obliterating. Don't do it. Sir Laurence Olivier used to ask anyone working on a project whether there was anything in it for him. If Sir Laurence could admit he wanted a job, am I going to pretend I don't?

After successfully freelancing for a long time, when I finally signed with an agent I thought my own agenting efforts were over. From the perspective of time and research I realize that because I was passive, didn't educate myself, and had abandoned all the job getting tasks I practiced before, I missed out on exploiting my success in a more meaningful way. I had this idea that you have a breakthrough and then everything just comes to you. Maybe for Julia Roberts, but even then, I doubt it. I just had no idea how the business works. It's a business, not a fairy tale. And it's a 24/7 business. That's the life you've chosen.

Some actors become angry when they have to tell their agents how to negotiate. They feel the agent is not doing his job if he has to be reminded to go for a particular kind of billing or per diem.

We all need encouragement and respond to reminders. I don't like to admit it, but I can almost always do better with prodding. I might not think so initially, but my extra efforts usually pay off.

If the agent does everything perfectly, great. But it's your career. It's up to you to know the union minimums and how to get your price up. It's up to you to figure out the billing you want and to help the agent get it. You are getting the 90%. Not only is it your responsibility, it's a way for you to be in control of your destiny in a business where it is too easy to feel tossed about by the whims of the gods.

Agents' Expectations

Before I talk about the agents' responsibilities, let's hear what agents expect from actors:

If I sign an actor for a year, I expect consistent callbacks. I expect, at least, growth. I'm not going to look at somebody's track record and say, "you've been out on fifty things here and you haven't booked a job; I don't think there's anything we can do here." It's difficult. It's very competitive. If I've believed in someone from the beginning, and if I see progress, if I see growth, and if I see the potential is still there, then I'm encouraged.

– Kenneth Kaplan, The Gersh Agency

I expect that they'll prepare the audition material ahead of time, they'll show up punctually, that they won't be afraid to go out on a limb and take some risks with the material, that they will return my phone calls promptly.

– Gary Epstein, Phoenix Artists

I expect my client to be on time, to be prepared, to be pleasant and to do the best job he can. Once I get you in the door, you are on your own. I think actors should not be afraid to take control of the situation. If they want to start over, they should say so. If they want to read different sides, they should ask for it. If they want to read another character, they should go for it. If they feel they were ignored, they should say so and not complain and whine to the agent.

The actor is a grown-up and casting directors are not demi-gods. They are people even though they have total control. I don't mean the actor has to complain, but he should make it known that he wasn't comfortable.

– Gary Krasny, The Krasny Office

A client will say, "are you angry with me because I didn't do so and so?" No. I'm giving you choices and opportunities. You make the decision and I'll go along with it. If I think it's a self-destructive point, I'll tell you. We can talk about it, but it's ultimately your decision.
— Tim Angle, Manager Shelter Entertainment Los Angeles

Remember, the agent puts his reputation on the line by sending you in and you put yours on the line by the quality of your work.

What the Actor Has a Right to Expect

All we want an agent to do for us is get us meetings for projects we are right for. This seemingly simple request requires of agents all the things that actors need to do: be informed and be professional, network, stay visible, and communicate.

As we maintain our credibility by giving consistently good readings, the agent maintains his credibility by building trust with the buyers. When he calls and says, "see K Callan, you won't be sorry," the casting director knows he won't.

If K Callan gets the job, the agent must be ready to do a wonderful job of negotiation, one that will make the actor (and the agent) happy and, at the same time, make the casting director feel he got a bargain.

The agent has all our responsibilities and more. The agent must maintain relationships with all of his clients and with the buyer. He must keep the buyers happy so that he can have return business.

If your agent can't get you in, the buyer won't get a chance to see your talent. Once in the buyer's presence, it's up to you to make your agent and the casting director look good by your brilliant work.

What the Actor Doesn't Have a Right to Expect

✓ It's not okay to call your agent at home other than in an emergency.
✓ It's not okay to drop by unannounced.

- ✓ It's not okay to expect your agent to deal with your personal problems.
- ✓ It's not okay to arrive late (or very early) for your meetings.
- ✓ It's not okay to expect to use the agent's phone for personal calls.
- ✓ It's not okay to hang around with the agent's auxiliary people when they are supposed to be working.
- ✓ It's not okay to bad-mouth the agent to others in the business. If you've got a gripe, take it up with the agent.
- ✓ It's not okay to interview new agents while your old agent thinks your relationship is swell.
- ✓ It's not okay to call and say: "What's happening?"
- ✓ It's not okay to expect the agent to put all the energy into the relationship.

A successful actor/agent relationship is no different than any other relationship. No one likes to be presumed upon.

Emotionally Prepared to Audition

If you are not feeling confident about yourself, go to class, talk to a friend, a therapist, whatever, but don't burden your agent with that information. Will he feel like using up his credibility telling them that you are the best actor since Meryl Streep when he knows you can't even get out of bed?

If you are not up to auditioning well, tell your agent and postpone or cancel the audition. You are not only not going to be performing well enough to get the job, but people will also lose confidence in you and in your agent's instincts. It will be harder to get the buyer to see you next time.

Staying In Touch

Keep in touch with your agent by being a good partner. Call with updates, a lead or to show him new pictures.

Give me a tool I can use. Actors need to do 50% and I will do the other 50%.
– Nancy Curtis, Harden Curtis Associates

Los Angeles manager Ric Beddingfield says actors should make it a point to be seen by their agents once a week. Although most agents agree grudgingly that actors and their agents need to be in constant contact, most also agree that they hate the phone call that says, "what's going on?" They translate that into "where's my appointment?"

It's like when you were little and your mom said, "what are you doing?" when she meant, "is your homework done?" If you think about it from that perspective, perhaps you'll find a way to have a conversation that does not make the agent feel defensive. If you are calling to say you've just gotten a good part in a showcase, or just began studying with a new teacher, or "hey, did you see the new play at The Public? It's great, don't miss it," the agent is going to be a lot happier to hear your voice or see your face.

When Laurie Walton was still an agent, she said,

The only thing I'm not enjoying is that actors call me daily. It's tough. I would never be unkind because I've been there, but on the other hand, I think a lot of them are taking advantage and that's the part I'm not enjoying because actors can really be annoying.

It's because everybody wants to work. I understand that hunger and need but it's interesting for me that they're not using their heads more and knowing that it's probably going to have the reverse effect.
– Laurie Walton

A Los Angeles agent put it succinctly, "my worst day is when I talk to more clients than buyers." Remember that while you are taking the negative step of whining to your agent, you are avoiding taking some kind of positive action for your career.

A non-obnoxious way to stay in touch presents itself when you drop off pictures and resumes. Call ahead and say that you are going to drop off new pictures and want to pop in. Once there, ask the receptionist if you can just stick your head in and say "hi." Late afternoon is best.

You can just be in the neighborhood and drop by to show a new wardrobe or haircut. Then be sure to do that; just poke your head in. Don't sit down unless asked and if asked stay no more than five minutes. Be adorable and leave.

If you are depressed and need to really talk, call ahead and see if your agent has time for you. Suggest a cup of coffee after work or, if he has time for a snack in the middle of the afternoon, you can bring goodies. Everyone is happy to see a treat in the late afternoon. Since most people bring in sweets, bring a basket of strawberries or blueberries. Agents will be happy to see something healthy.

Make the effort to speak to everyone in the office and call them by their names. Get to know your agents and their support staff on a person-to-person basis. Learn something about each one of them and take notes so you can establish personal relationships. You'll be able to say something that is not about you and/or the business. That will make all of you feel more comfortable.

At one time, I discouraged e-mails for staying in touch, but some agents say an email or Facebook post is a good way to stay in touch. You'll need to ask your partner what works for him.

It takes two energy-expending components to make any merger work. The agent must work hard for you all of the time and you need to deliver all of the time. If you don't stay abreast of what's in town, what shows are on television that might use your type, what you got paid for your last job, which casting directors you have met, who your fans are, and/or if you are late or ill-prepared for appointments, the agent is going to get cranky.

If he doesn't drop you, he'll stop working for you. Worse, you'll get work anyway and he won't feel able to drop you. He'll just hate you.

If you are diligent, do everything you can do for your own career, and consistently give your agent leads that he doesn't follow up on, then you're going to get cranky and leave. It takes two.

Wrap Up

Upon Signing

✓ officially notify the previous agent that you are leaving

✓ visit new agent with pictures, resumes, DVDs, CD/Director contacts

✓ meet everyone in the office

✓ make map of where everyone sits

✓ send necessary letters to unions

The Actor's 90%

✓ stay professionally informed

✓ network

✓ follow through

✓ communicate

✓ make informed suggestions

✓ continue study

✓ check for messages often

✓ return calls promptly

✓ stay visible

✓ be loyal

✓ prepare for auditions carefully

✓ be punctual

The Agents 10%

✓ arrange meetings with casting directors, producers and directors

✓ arrange auditions

✓ negotiate

✓ network

✓ maintain credibility

✓ communicate

✓ make informed decisions

✓ stay professionally informed

✓ return phone calls promptly

✓ guide career

chapter 12

To Leave or Not to Leave

Deciding to get a divorce is a weighty matter whether it's a regular marriage or a business marriage no matter whose idea it is.

If you are leaving your agent of your own accord, the most common reasons are usually that you're not getting auditions or you've had a lucky break.

There may be many reasons why you aren't getting auditions that have nothing to do with your agent, however, so don't be rash. You might have gained or lost weight and now no one knows what to do with you. You may be traveling into a new age category and have not yet finished the journey. You might be getting stale and need to study. You might be having personal problems at home that are reflected in your work (after all, it's the life energy that fuels our talent and craft). The business might have changed, beautiful people may be in (or out).

Can you list projects that had parts for you on which you were not seen? And were there really parts for you? You have to be right for a part not only physically and energetically but also on an appropriate career level as well.

Maybe you felt your agent didn't work hard enough. Maybe your expectations were out of line. Maybe you were lazy. Maybe you didn't keep his enthusiasm high enough. Maybe he was a goof-off. Maybe you were.

But, if there are no parts in your category right now, a new agent can't change that. He might send you out on auditions you're not right for and make you feel busy, but you're still not going to get a job you are not right for.

Agents tell me the number one reason that a working actor leaves one prestigious, credible agent for another is that the actor sees his career in a different venue.

If he's on soaps, he wants to be on primetime. If he's a television star, he wants to do films. When an actor becomes a star in one area of the business, that probably means many people are telling the actor how terrific he is and that now he can do anything. That may not be true.
— Anonymous Agent

Right behind upward mobility, the next most common reason an actor leaves is because he's not getting auditions.

For an agent and talent to continue together when nothing is happening, it's bad for both sides. Never feel bad about leaving an agency and an agent should never feel bad about dropping a talent. Sometimes I'll have a talent and they're with me for six months and nothing happens, but they try another agent and somehow the chemistry works there and something happens. Whatever that agency's connections are are more in line with that particular talent's abilities.
— Aur-Aelion Israel, Almond Talent Agency Los Angeles

Every agent has different contacts. An agent may have great theatre contacts and no film contacts but tells the actor he does. If you were that actor and the agent didn't get you a film audition for a year, you'd be getting the sense that one of you didn't have the chops to get you in.

Maybe your agent is not out there pushing for you. How can you tell if it's just not your turn or if the agent is off playing the horses? You could drop off some pictures at the office and see if he's there and if the phone is ringing for anyone. You could look at his client list on IMDbPro and see if anyone else on the list is working.

Maybe you and your agent have different ideas regarding your potential. If this topic was not discussed up front, both of you may be feeling disappointed and misunderstood. This is a legitimate problem.

Most of the time, when someone leaves, it's mutual. The bottom line is that it is the actor's career. If he is not happy, then it's up to him to say, "can I have a meeting because it's been too long?" And then we will say, "what have you seen that you weren't up for? Or what have you heard of?"

He might mention a project that he wasn't in on and we'll pull it out and see that on that project they were looking for stars or younger or whatever. As soon as we talk about it, the problem is usually over. It's important, though, to have the conversation.

– Ellie Goldberg, Kerin-Goldberg Associates

I just had an argument with a manager who was upset because I was dropping his client. I said, "I don't understand why you are upset. It's been a year and nothing has happened. They'll be better off someplace else. Why wouldn't you want to try something else?"

– Aur-Aelion Israel, Almond Talent Agency Los Angeles

If the agent screws up a job, I think you should leave. If you don't get any appointments and you think you should be getting appointments, then you should move on to someone who is excited. If the agent doesn't take your phone calls, that's really a sign that there is something wrong. Sometimes you just have to get a fresh outlook. It works both ways.

– Gary Krasny, The Krasny Office

The Lucky Break

Perhaps your level of achievement in the business has risen. You have now, through diligent work and study and possibly a lucky break, become an actor of greater stature than your agent and you feel you have outgrown him. And maybe you have.

I have to be honest and look at a performer's career I started and took up the road for six years and who's now making millions of dollars a picture for WME. If I could have done that, then I would have done that. Maybe I could do it now. But, obviously, if I could have done it then, then I would have.

– Martin Gage, BRS/Gage Talent Agency

And when you have a lucky break, sometimes the agent who spent his time and energy developing you gets burned. LA agent, Jimmy Cota has retired, but he knows:

Every agent has four or five horror stories about all they've done for somebody and then the person comes in and says, "I know you did a lot for me, but it wasn't enough. Someone's going to do more." Those are the ones that kill you, that keep you awake at night, that make you say, "Hey, maybe I should get out of this business."
– Jimmy Cota

An agent told me that a newly visible client came into his office, sat down and said, "I'm so excited. I know you'll be happy for me. I'm now so successful that WME wants me."

Can you believe it? This actor wants the agent whose hard work, contacts and persistence helped him realize his dreams to be happy that the work is going to pay off for WME?

There's no way an independent agent can defend himself about a suddenly visible, successful client leaving the agency for a corporate agency without sounding like sour grapes. We took an actress from zero to being very visible and very successful on a television show. She left because she "wanted to do more movies." In the last two months with us, we got her two movies. She's now been with the corporate agency for ten months and hasn't done a movie.

When she left, I said, "You are definitely screwing me no matter what you want to call it. I stood by you for five years when nobody would help you. I only hope you're screwing me for a reason. I hope five years from now, you can look back and know why you screwed me. You traded me off for something and the question is: 'Did you trade off the last person who didn't see you as a dollar sign to enter a world where they only value you as a dollar sign?'"
– Anonymous Agent

And then there are those moments when the actor's career loses momentum. One minute he's hot and the next moment he's not. He didn't necessarily do anything special to get himself un-hot (frequently getting hot works the same way).

At a smaller agency, a downturn in your career won't necessarily make you persona non grata, but at the big agencies, it might be difficult for you to get your agent on the phone.

When a client of mine doesn't get work, I just figure the people who are doing the hiring are morons. I know when I take on a client that it's for life. I have so much faith in my own taste that I would never lose faith in a client.
– Phil Adelman, BRS/Gage Talent Agency

The larger agencies are not in the business to handle less profitable jobs, so they either drop you or their lack of interest finally tells you that you're no longer on their level.

This is the moment when you might be sorry you left that small agent who worked so hard to get you started and engineered the big break for you. Will he want to see you now? He might. He might not. It depends on how you handled it when leaving as well as the momentum of your career at that point.

The bottom line is that actor/agent relationships are like any other relationship: as long as it's mutually rewarding everyone is happy; when it's not, things must change.

Telling/Shopping

Before you start looking for a new agent, you must make a decision about telling your current agent you are going to leave. Most actors are hesitant not only because they are embarrassed and guilty, but also because they feel the agent might stop submitting them and the actor would be left unrepresented while he is shopping.

First of all, I doubt the agent would want to forego the commissions due on any new jobs. Second, if he wants to keep you, this is his chance to demonstrate you are making a mistake and he really is the best agent in the world, after all.

We're all actors and we want to be liked. Bringing up the subject of leaving isn't fun, but for me, when I did it, not as bad as my fantasy. I just said I was unhappy about the way a couple of things had been handled and thinking of returning to my former agent though I hadn't spoken to him yet. My agent at the time said, "Thank you for your candor. If you want to go back to David and he wants you, I'll understand. If you decide not to, I'll forget we ever had this conversation."

What a relief. And I can't tell you how virtuous I felt.

A plus for telling your agent is you don't have to worry about word getting back to him prematurely that you are doing research or actually interviewing. Not only that, any agents and/or casting directors will notice that you don't play both ends against the middle.

Every agent I questioned said they would never leave an actor without any representation while he was shopping.

If it is too late for a talk or you talked and it didn't help, at least be gracious. Even though it might be uncomfortable, get on with it. There is no need for long recriminations. No excuses. Not "My wife thinks" or "My manager thinks."

No, it should be "I've decided that I am going to make a change. I appreciate all the work you have done for me. I will miss seeing you, but it just seems like the time to make a change. For whatever reason, it's just not working. I hope we'll see each other again.'

Whatever. You don't need to be phony. If you don't appreciate what the guy has done and don't think he's done any work, just skip it. Talk about the fact that you think the relationship is not, or is no longer, mutually rewarding. Be honest and leave both of you with some dignity. Remember, you may see this person again. With some distance between you, you might even remember why you signed with him in the first place. Don't close doors.

If you are leaving because your fortunes have risen, it is even harder. The agent will be upset to see you and your money leave. Also, your new found success has probably come from his efforts as well as yours. But if you are really hot and feel only CAA or WME can handle you, leave you must.

Tell your agent you wish it were another way but the vicissitudes of the business indicate that at a certain career level, CAA and their peers have more information, clout and other stars to bargain with, and you want to go for it.

If you handle it well and if your agent is smart, he will leave the door open. It has happened to him before and it will happen to him again. That doesn't make it hurt less, but this is business. He will probably just shake his head and tell his friends you have gone crazy: "This isn't the same Mary I always knew. Success has gone to her head."

The agent has to find some way to handle it just as you would if he were firing you. It will not be easy to begin a new business relationship, but you are hot right now and the world is rosy.

If you haven't notified your old agent, do so now. Do it in person and do it graciously. Make it a point to speak to, and thank all your agents and everyone else in the office for their efforts, pick up your pictures, tapes, etc., and leave. Send the necessary letters to the unions.

That's the advice I used to give, but there are other perspectives:

If you are breaking up with your agent, sometimes actors think this is like a regular relationship coming to an end. It is a relationship, but a business relationship. I've had clients say I want to meet up with you and I set aside time and drive across town to have coffee and they're ending the relationship. Well, why waste my time like that? Why did you call me across town to tell me this, you could have saved me an hour with just an email. Say "Hey, I'm going with another agent, thank you for everything." And I thank them for everything and that's it. Young actors feel like it's a dating thing.
– Aur-Aelion Israel, Almond Talent Agency Los Angeles

Not all agents feel that way though. I think it depends on the length and depth of your partnership, how long you've been together and so on. You'll have to weigh it for yourself.

Jumping ship every six months (which a lot of actors do) only serves to hurt the actor because everybody knows about it and it shows that the actor can't necessarily get a job because something's wrong and it's not because of the agent.

– Gary Krasny, The Krasny Office

I would be very upset if someone with whom I've had a long relationship fired me by letter. I think it would be the ultimate rudeness, ingratitude, lack of appreciation for the work I've done. Get past the guilt, the embarrassment. I'm owed a certain consideration. Deal with it. I understand the difficulty, but that's not an excuse.

– Phil Adelman, BRS/Gage Talent Agency

So be a grown-up. Your agent deserves the courtesy of a personal meeting. Go in and talk to him.

The Dumpee

If you are the one being dumped, that's depressing. Although there is no way being dumped can feel good, once you get over the pain of rejection, assessing the situation can put a whole different light on it.

There are many reasons that you may find yourself agentless. Your agent might have moved to another agency and was not allowed to bring you or he may have decided to retire or you may be going through a down time and just not be able to carry your weight financially.

Agents sometimes drop clients for bad behavior ("life's too short") or lack of communication. Sometimes it's because the agent's list has gotten too big/costly and the agent needs to trim.

At many agencies, each agent is responsible for his portion of the rent, phone bill, messengers, etc. The agent has to pay his bills, too, and though he may love you personally, he may make a business decision to bet on someone else for a change and you are out in the cold.

I recently worked with a well known actress who told me that at a down point in her career, her agent had dumped her. She said that although she was crushed in the moment, that ultimately it was a good thing because she had to face that representation is about business and not friendship. That bit of information freed her to make the best decision for herself further down the line, when she ended up leaving a later agent because she just felt it wasn't working.

When things aren't working in your career anyway and then your agents severs your relationship also, it's difficult to handle, but if you look at what happened, accept your responsibility in it and move forward, you are not only stronger for it, you're smarter.

Wrap Up

Questionable Reasons for Leaving
✓ no recent work
✓ agent disinterest

Better Remedies than Leaving Agent
✓ learn to communicate better with your agent
✓ take a class, study with a coach

Speak to Agent
✓ before things get bad
✓ before interviewing new agents

Clear-Cut Reasons for Leaving
✓ lack of communication
✓ differing goals
✓ personality differences
✓ sudden career change

When You Are Dumped
✓ can be painful and depressing
✓ can be a valuable learning experience

chapter _13

Managers

Although more and more actors in Los Angeles are choosing to have managers, that's not the case in New York. I think the reason has to do with how difficult it is for newly arrived actors in LA to connect with agents, so they turn to managers as an alternative. It's difficult to get representation in New York, as well, but actors in Manhattan appear to be a grittier bunch and are better about just hunkering down and agenting themselves for the grind until a credible agent might be interested.

In any event, there are conflicting views as to the desirability of having a manager. Twice in my career (once in New York and once in Los Angeles), I had a manager. Not only did the service not enhance my career, but for the entire duration of each contract, I had no work at all. But that's me, I'm a character person; if you're a young leading man/woman, you could have a different experience or if you're a big name at a big agency, you might really want/need a manager.

Many feel having a manager increases their access to work. It may. It may not. Having a manager is really just having a second agent who is not regulated by the state or any of the unions, who may or may not have more contacts than your agent and may or may not be able to help you focus your presentation, but *will* cost you additional money.

If you seek a manager because you cannot get an agent, I'm wondering how you think the manager is going to help you. If the agent did not see anything marketable, is the manager going to create you? It could happen, but I'd want some proof of that manager's access and developmental skills. Some managers latch onto every new face in town, hoping that somehow one of them will hit.

Beverly Robin Green is an entertainment attorney in San Francisco. Although she works mainly in the music field, her words about managers are valid for managers of actors:

Artists often say they would like to put together a professional "team" of a manager, agent, and attorney. They ask me where they can find the manager or agent. That is a good goal and a good question. It opens up a lot of other questions about what the artist is really looking for, and what the artist has to offer. The different roles that managers and agents play in the music business are difficult to define. They even vary widely in their own categories and from situation to situation, and this can be confusing. Also, what an artist wants may simply not be available to them at this point in their career, especially with respect to managers and agents, who usually work strictly on a commission basis. Another problem is that many of these people simply do not want to bother working for an artist until the artist has already gotten a record contract or is otherwise already taking off in their career. This creates a "Catch 22" situation for the aspiring artist.

On a practical level, in selecting a manager, you need to define what you need the manager for and see if that role fits the person you are considering. A lot of times people say they want a manager to get them gigs (wrong, but often done) or to get them a record deal (in California anyway), but a manager who is unknown and inexperienced is not going to have the knowledge, connections or reputation to be of much help in this regard.
– OnStage Magazine[20]

On the other hand, some excellent agents, upset by agency defections and what they deem unfair/unregulated competition from managers, are choosing to dump their agency franchises and become managers themselves.

Aside from the business machinations, however, the events of the past two weeks also have had an impact on a personal level. Hyper-caffeinated, mega-testosteroned, over-compensated agents are asking themselves: Why am I in this line of work? Given the existing climate, are alternative careers more intriguing? Would it even be more rewarding to be a manager rather than an agent?

Paul Young, who runs Principato Young, reminded me this week that managers don't wear suits, don't have to cope with complicated bureaucracies or adjust budgets to placate private equity investors. They can be more involved with the creative process, and serve as executive producers on projects they develop with clients. In short, they can have a stake in the game.

— Variety[21]

These agents turned managers have credibility and in their earlier careers existed at a very high level, but those who just woke up one day and decided to call themselves managers? I wonder.

I think a manager that is connected and in love with you, could surely enhance your career. But, if you're going to choose a manager, do the research and make sure that's the manager you're getting.

If you just graduated from one of the Leagues and scored well in their showcases, many agents and managers may be giving you their cards. You have options. You don't need a manager. Credible, helpful, respected agents want you. You don't need a manager to help you sort the offers. You've already been groomed by your expensive school.

It's possible that a manager could get to you before you meet any agents and say, "Hey, don't bother meeting any agents, I'll take care of that for you when you are my client."

I see where they are coming from on that, because if you are going to have a manager, one of the services you might expect from the manager would be his input into your agent selection. However if you never meet and have experience with an agent, how will you make an informed decision regarding the need for a manager?

There are managers out there who wine and dine actors after the showcases and tell them not to meet with agents themselves and not to return their phone calls, particularly mid-level agents. Those actors might really be missing out. They should be meeting with the agents and making their own decisions. It's possible they don't even need a manager.

— Gary Krasny, The Krasny Office, Inc.

Meet with anyone who calls and listen to what they have to say. Only by gathering information and experiences can you make an informed choice.

Don't be in a hurry. Managers are all salesmen and make brilliant impressions. You will be tempted to sign in the moment, but you need to do research and weigh all your offers. The right manager who is connected and passionate about your career can definitely make a difference, but so could the right agent. Why pay an extra commission?

When Julia Roberts came to New York (already connected because of her already famous brother, Eric), her manager, Bob McGowan, uncovered a part for her in the movie *Satisfaction*. The part called for a musician, so Bob enrolled Roberts in a crash course and enticed William Morris into repping her for the job.

So, if we had McGowan for a manager and happened to look like Julia Roberts and have her charisma, who knows what could happen? And what did happen? Ultimately, Roberts dropped McGowan and opted for WMA and no manager, choosing to not have any more layers between herself and her work.

But McGowan made that job happen. Would Julia have opted for the crash course or even have known that was needed? If you luck into a manager with McGowan's taste, creativity and access who helps shape you, it would certainly be worth it.

Managers Can't Legally Procure Work

Although the law has rarely been enforced, managers are not legally allowed to procure work. That's the business of those people who have licenses from the state: you know, the agents.

Actress Jennifer Lopez has filed a petition with the California Labor Commissioner accusing her former manager of violating the state's Talent Agency Act by procuring employment on her behalf.

The primary charge centers on whether Benny Medina was acting as her agent. Because Medina allegedly procured and negotiated work for her, the petition is requesting that all oral and engagement contracts she had with Handprint be voided. Those contracts saw her pay 10% of earnings from movies and television, 15% of

her music, recording and publishing earnings, and 10% of her earnings from ancillary activities, including fashion and cosmetic interests.
– Hollywood Reporter[22]

Actress Nia Vardalos won a similar lawsuit against her ex-manager:

The state court judge has refused to hear a challenge from Nia Vardalos' ex-manager to California's law barring managers from acting as talent agents. Tuesday's ruling by Los Angeles Superior Court Judge Judith Chirlin sets the stage for the state labor commission to go ahead with a proceeding next week against Marathon Entertainment for performing as an unlicensed talent agent for Vardalos.

The management company sued Vardalos in January for failing to pay 15% commission from her earnings from the hit comedy feature, "My Big Fat Greek Wedding," which she wrote and starred in.
– Daily Variety[23]

No one believes that Lopez and Vardalos suddenly found religion and don't want to be in business with someone who is breaking the law. The lawsuits look like a way to avoid paying commissions and get out of a contract. The fact remains that it's illegal for a manager to procure work for you. The Association of Talent Agents webpage agrees:

The job of the ATA agent is to create opportunities, procure and negotiate employment for clients, and counsel them in the development of their careers. Agents in most states must be licensed by the state, city or appropriate governing body. Managers are not regulated nor are they required to have a license. Under law, managers may not procure employment for artists or negotiate without a licensed agent, and any person who renders Agent services without a license may have their contract invalidated and be forced to relinquish any commissions paid.
– agentassociation.com/frontdoor/faq.cfm

And if he's not going to procure work for you, why would you be wanting a manager? There are other reasons, believe it or not.

When It Makes Sense To Have A Manager

Managers are a definite plus for child actors who need guidance and whose families have no show business background. A manager usually places the child with an agent, monitors auditions and sometimes accompanies the child to meetings and auditions.

If you are entering the business and need help with pictures, resumes, image, etc., managers can be helpful. There are, however, agents who consider this part of their service.

When you are at a conglomerate agency and it's intimidating and time consuming to keep in touch with 20 agents, it would be advantageous, perhaps necessary, to have a manager in your corner, though I was interested to note that Matthew McConaughey doesn't have a manager and has an agent he feels he can depend on to fight his battles at CAA:

That question of agent versus agency also came up at a 2014 CAA retreat in Carlsbad, Calif. There, star client Matthew McConaughey took the stage in a giant conference room to be interviewed by Maha Dakhil, a senior literary agent.

During the conversation, Dakhil said: "So let me ask you a question: What's more important, your agent or the agency?" McConaughey, 45, whose longtime agent, Jim Toth, was sitting in the audience, then began what a source who was present says was a palpably uncomfortable monologue. "Are you kidding me?" McConaughey is said to have answered. "My agent, not my agency. My agent is the one who fights for me every day." As the crowd shifted awkwardly, the source says the actor went further, saying: "Don't think I don't know what's going on here. You guys represent my competition — Brad Pitt, Tom Cruise, George Clooney. They're all fighting for the jobs I want, and my agent is fighting for me." (Others present refute this account, and McConaughey couldn't be reached for comment.)
– The Hollywood Reporter[24]

Some people want a manager because they want to change agents and it *is* easier when you have a manager, because the manager does all the research, calling and rejecting of the former agent. If agent changing is the only reason you have engaged the services of a manager, it's an expensive antidote to one uncomfortable meeting.

If you have the credits to support getting a good agent, you can do that on your own. If you don't, the manager can't create them.

I have a few friends who feel the presence of a manager enhanced their careers at least momentarily. One in particular said her agents were considering dropping her, so she and the manager decided to make her more attractive to the agents by getting some jobs themselves. They read The Breakdown and the actress delivered her own submissions to the casting offices.

If the manager got a call for an appointment, the actress went in and if she got the job, they called the agent to make the deal. The agent became more enthusiastic about the actress for a while, but ultimately dropped her. The agent's earlier indifference signaled what he had already decided: that the actress was no longer appropriate for his list. In that case, the manager, though helpful, only delayed the inevitable. That story is doubly sad because it illustrates that the manager really had no contacts to add to the equation.

Another food group that does particularly well with managers are comedy actors. There are managers whose main job is checking out the comedy/improv clubs for new talent and helping them develop.

If you're in that group, research a comic you like. See who the manager is and who else is on that list.

Agent Relationship vs. Manager Relationship

If you go with a manager, you might forego a personal relationship with your agent. If you don't like your agent, but he's effective, maybe you don't want to deal with him either, so a manager is a good choice. But if you've had a fruitful, long standing relationship with your agent, it will be difficult for both of you to now speak only through the manager.

I'm still anti-manager for most young people entering the business with nothing to sell unless that manager is going to develop the actor. And even then, entering the system takes about three years anyway.

Commit to developing yourself. Be diligent with your study of the business and your craft. Be a sponge. Look at other actors pictures. Note who is working where. Look up their agents in IMDbPro. Study voice, dance, acting, dialect. Produce work with your friends. Commit to 5 minutes a week online. You will get better. You will ripen. It might feel comforting to have a cheerleader while you are doing this, but this is a service you can give yourself. There are some managers who demand 15% of the actors day job. Seriously?

I continue to be negative about the many newly-minted-uncredentialed-managers haunting showcases to sign new young beautiful people and then wait for the self motivated to succeed on their own and then take a piece of the action. The purpose of a manager is to manage. That means you have so many jobs that you can't keep them straight and they have to fight off the press for you. Wait until you have those problems?

If you can forge a relationship with a credible agent, that would be my choice for you. But I know that's hard and I also know you're not going to listen to me, so at least let me give you some advice.

Hidden Agendas

In addition to their goal of getting clients work, some managers use their power with their stars as an entrée to life as a producer. They hold back access to their clients if they are not given producer credit.

Network and studio brass have privately complained of what they saw as a conflict of interest that pushed their budgets higher with nothing to show for it, other than a relationship with the person with access to the star actor, writer or director. The late Pat McQueeney never exploited her position:

Many talent agents and studio executives believe that managers should focus on managing clients, not on producing their work.

Of course it's extortion, said Pat McQueeney, a manager who has represented Harrison Ford for 27 years. McQueeney has always refused to put her name on any of her sole client's movies. I don't approve of it, she said. It's double-dipping to be paid a double commission as a manager and a producer.

According to McQueeney, people have said, "Produce with us," trying to bribe me by giving me a job I don't want, in order to secure Ford's commitment to a project. Because everybody's dream in this town is to become a producer, I feel they (managers) use their clients to benefit themselves and further their own careers.

– The Los Angeles Times[25]

Some resent the imposition of a personal manager hired just because of his or her star access. "It's very difficult to say no [to a manager's producer credit] without offending the talent," Tolan noted, even though in 95% of the cases, the manager brings nothing to the table.

Erwin Moore [a personal manager] admitted the conflict of interest question has come up many times, but never as a personal issue with me or my clients, he said.

When the dust has settled, people will come back to the realization that we're here to serve a purpose on behalf of our clients. But the dust won't settle any time soon. With managers growing more and more involved as producers, expect more complications and litigation in the future.

–The Hollywood Reporter[26]

Agents must be franchised by the entertainment unions and the state, displaying at least a modicum of track record, honesty and skills before they are certified. They may only charge 10% and may only sign new clients to one year if they are SAG franchised. Those with ATA agreements have differing rules.

The National Conference of Personal Managers does not endorse the newly established SAG-AFTRA Personal Manager Code of Ethics and Conduct.

There is no certifying group overseeing the activity or contracts of managers. Commissions and terms of service are totally negotiable so if you are signing with a manager, insist on a one year contract to start and if you are a member, SAG-AFTRA lawyers to go over the contract with you.

NCOPM appears to be the only group collecting personal managers and, to me, doesn't appear to be a comprehensive list of managers if you compare it to managers listed at IMDbPro.com. NCOPM's website: ncopm.com/about/ncopm-code-ethics.

What Do Managers Think Their Job Is?

From The National Conference Of Personal Managers website:

First, let's state what a personal manager is not. A personal manager is not an agent (whose role is to obtain employment). A personal manager is not a publicist (whose role is to generate publicity). Nor is a personal manager an attorney (whose role is to provide legal counsel). And, a personal manager is not a business manager (whose role is to provide accounting, investment, and other financial services).

A personal manager advises and counsels talent and personalities in the entertainment industry.

Personal managers have the expertise to find and develop new talent and create opportunities for those artists which they represent. Personal managers act as liaison between their clients and both the public and the theatrical agents, publicists, attorneys, business managers, and other entertainment industry professionals which provide services to the personal manager's clients.

– ncopm.com.

Even though the NCOPM says managers "have the expertise...", there is no governing body that certifies this to be true. You could decide right now to be a manager, hang a shingle, announce your new business to the trades, and wait for the 8x10s. So just as you would in any business situation, ask questions. It's difficult to withstand a full court press from someone who professes to love you and want to help you, but find out if this person has the credentials to do that.

A highly visible friend of mine recently lost a job because her manager discouraged her from speaking to her agent. The actress lost the job over money that would make no difference in her lifestyle. The agent might have prevailed in the negotiation.

The job was in a show that is now a huge hit and would have given real momentum to my friend's career. I kept saying, "Why don't you call your agent and ask what is happening?" Her reply? "I don't want to make my manager mad."

On those two unsuccessful occasions when I did have a manager, the thing I liked least was that I was not supposed to talk to my agent myself. That was then and this is now. If I had a connected powerful manager in my corner who was in love with me and saying my name, I'm pretty sure I could be happy just dealing with him. ; -)

Researching Managers
Check out managers the same way you do agents. Google specific name for online information. Ask friends if they have heard of anyone who has a manager who has enhanced their careers. Check out IMDbPro's Companies tab for management companies. You'll see a list in order of importance. When you click on the company, you'll see staff and clients, just as you do with agents.

Watch films and television zeroing on shows that use people like you, then research actors from the show on IMDbPro to see if they have a manager and who that is. A young actress told me she polled 60 managers this way and end up with a top drawer management team.

If you know any casting directors well enough to ask, ask for recommendations.

If you do set up a meeting, be prepared to ask how the manager got into the business, what casting directors he has relationships with. You should check out the list of his clients at IMDbPro before the meeting. You might ask how long a particular person has been with them and try to judge if the manager had a hand in developing the talent or the actor joined the manager pretty far along in his career.

Don't be short-sighted. Have faith in yourself. Whether you are choosing an agent or a manager, don't just take the first person who shows some interest. Even though it may not seem that way right now, you have assets to protect: your face and your career. Many say, "Well, so what if someone wants to charge me 25%? Right now, I am making nothing, if I make money, give this person 25%."

That's fine today while you aren't making any money, but when you do, and you have a manager that is taking 25%, an agent who is taking 10% and Uncle Sam taking from a third to 50% depending on your tax bracket, you will be taking home very little money from all your work.

A few agencies told me that since most of their jobs are now booked at scale + 10% even for actors with Emmys and Tonys, that they have to have a bigger client list in order to pay their rent and that maybe a manager is a good idea.

Wrap Up

Managers

✓ can provide access
✓ can provide guidance
✓ illegal for them to procure work
✓ take a larger percentage than agents
✓ are not governed by industry standard contracts
✓ do your research
✓ real function is to manage something

chapter _14

Comedy/Solo Shows

Amy Schumer, Judd Apatow, Bill Hader, Melissa McCarthy and Bob
Odenkirk are all performers and stand-ups who crossed over into films
and television. Today, added to that list are other performers who write,
stage and star in their own webseries and solo-person shows. Assaulting
films and television via these avenues has become so profitable that no
less than ICM Partners has put together a team of people who actually
develop the careers of budding comedy talents.

*"For years, we've only handled established comedians because we didn't really have
the infrastructure to service (unknown) people," says Steve Levine, who heads ICM's
music and live performance division. "Now, we've put together a committed group
here who use the resources of the whole company" to build careers, he said.*
— Hollywood Reporter[27]

But how do you enter the field? Judd Apatow's excellent book *Sick
in the Head* is the perfect place to start your research. When Judd was 15,
he managed to interview many of his comic idols by calling their
publicists for interviews for his radio show. He neglected to mention his
age or that the radio station was in his high school.

I particularly appreciated Jerry Seinfield answer to Judd's question
as to how you get steady work:

*Well, you audition. You start off at three in the morning and you fight your way
through the order by doing better than the guy they put on before you. Then the next
night they put you ahead of him. Then you try to do better than that guy. But if
you're good, people notice you. That's the greatest thing about comedy. If you've got
talent, it's unmistakable. No one misses it and you don't have to wait around for a
break. It's very easy to get a break. It's very hard to be good though.*
— Sick in the Head[28]

Can just anyone be successful as a stand-up?

I wouldn't assume that just because you are a comedic actor that you can do stand-up. Soap opera people try to do stand-up. Most of them, because they are so pretty, have not lived that angst ridden life that comics have. It becomes a frivolous version of comedy. The first thing you want to establish with an actor that is going into comedy is: Do they have a natural feel for it? Do they have comedic rhythm for it? There are many actors who are wonderful with comedy, but can't do stand-up. You need the stage time.

We've definitely steered toward a very personality oriented comic. A charismatic style comic. The Tonight Show *might use a comic because they're a very good comic in terms of their writing: a structural comic who writes a perfect setup and a punch line. Some of those comics wouldn't crossover into a sitcom because they might just be joke tellers. We want somebody who is a very full bodied character a la Roseanne, Tim Allen, Seinfeld. The development and casting people are looking for that. They are already walking in with a character. Some comics have stronger skills in that area.*

– Bruce Smith, Omnipop Management

Jay Leno talked about his seven year rule in Franklyn Ajaye's book of interviews with other comics:

"I've always told comedians that if you can do this for seven years, I mean physically make it to the stage for seven years, you'll always make a living. If you've been in the business longer than seven years and you're not successful, there's probably another reason. Sex, dope, alcohol, drugs - - you just couldn't physically get to the stage. Sam Kinison is sort of an example. He was funny, hilarious, but near the end he couldn't get to the stage anymore. No matter how popular you are, promoters are not going to rehire you if you miss gigs."
– Comic Insights[29]

A lot of comedy clubs across the country have closed, but there are still some in the Northeast, so it's easier to keep a comic working there as they start to develop. The more stage time they have, the better they become. We encourage them to get into acting classes, not to become actors, but just to start. We want to know what their long range goals are. In order for a comic to become popular, he needs television exposure. If you can support that with a strong act, you're going to have a good career.

– Tom Ingegno, Omnipop Management

A comedic person has to have the backing of theatrical training, otherwise you're looking at a personality-oriented project. Many stand-ups came out of theatre and did stand-up as a means of survival.

– Steve Tellez/Innovative Artists

I would say to really know whether you have any place in the comedy business at all, that you would have to give yourself at least two years. Less than that is not enough. The first year you'll spend just trying to get your name around, trying to get people to know who you are so they will give you some stage time.

It's a long trip. Just like an actor. Don't seek representation with five minutes of material. You need to keep working. The next thing to do is to try to get work in road clubs. It's very important to get the experience. There is limited experience if you just stay in one city.

– Bruce Smith, Omnipop Management

The personal appearance agents that I spoke to supported what I learned from theatrical and literary agents: no one is interested in one-shot representation.

If you get a guest shot on a comedy show and call a credible agent with that as an entrée, he will probably talk to you. But if you don't have a track record of comedy credits the agent is not going to be interested. 10% of one episode isn't enough to get you on his list and share all his introductions and hard work.

If you have written a solo show and Disney is interested, that might be interesting to a stand-up agent. However development deals go south with regularity and if you don't already have a stand-up career going for yourself, credible personal appearance agents are not going to be interested. They want people who have been playing clubs in and out of town and have the stage time and some good material.

Stand-up and performance artist shows are a bonafide way to be entrepreneurial about the business, but there are no short-cuts to theatrical/comedic maturity. You gotta do the time.

Wrap Up
Stand-ups
- ✓ need fifteen to twenty minutes of material to begin
- ✓ need a persona
- ✓ should have theatrical training
- ✓ gotta do the stage time

Solo Shows
- ✓ needs resonance
- ✓ avoid vanity piece

chapter 15

Children in the Business

I don't think life as a child actor is a good deal for kids. You only get one shot at being a child and being taken care of. If you blow that, you are up a creek.

The tabloids make a lot of money running stories on the messed-up lives of former child actors. Lindsay Lohan anyone? Justin Bieber? I know you think you and/or your children could never have those problems. Maybe you won't. But at least think seriously about the possibilities before you take the next steps. If your child is paying your rent, the balance of power tips and there is no more family hierarchy.

That said, my interview with stage mother/manager, now retired children's agent, Judy Savage shot all my arguments full of holes.

Kids who have problems in the business came from dysfunctional families in the first place. It's not necessarily that the business goes to the children's heads, it goes to the parents' heads. I don't think the number of showbiz kids who become messed up is any greater than the general public, but you hear about them because they are so visible and they have a little more money for drugs.
– Judy Savage, The Savage Agency Los Angeles

Judy's philosophy explains why her clients and her own kids ended up not only working, but being productive grown-ups as well:

I think it's a great business and that you can pay for your braces, your caps, your car, your wedding, your house, and hopefully go on in the business or in some other aspect of life with a good start. Treat it as a hobby that you are lucky enough to get paid for, it's not going to go on forever. You can count on your two hands the number of actors whose careers go on for 40-50 years. The average career is five years for all members of Screen Actors Guild.
– Judy Savage, The Savage Agency Los Angeles

Elizabeth Taylor's life as a child actor is not one she recommended:

Looking back, I think I missed not having a childhood, not going to a regular school. I had a lot of fathers and avuncular friends on the set. They were great. They used to throw me around and play baseball with me and sneak me candy and comic books. But it wasn't the same as having peers, and I think I would advise parents of child actors not to push it. It's a hard life for a child not to have a childhood. Its rough.
– The Los Angeles Times[30]

The decision is yours, but if you do decide to pursue a career for your child or if you are a child reading this, remember, it's easier to maintain your balance when you are a working actor, than if you are a star.

You Don't Have to Be in New York or Los Angeles
I get mail as well as questions on the Internet from parents and kids asking me how they can get started in the business if they don't live in New York, Chicago or Los Angeles. Judy Savage's story is a good example of how to go about it.

Summering at her folks summer home in a lakeside Michigan summer musical area, housewife-mother-pre-med student, Savage, pregnant with her third child, was the mother of a talented nine-year-old son. She was told by a New York casting director, "Sell your house. Sell your car. Take this child to New York."

Judy didn't see herself uprooting her family so drastically, but when she got back to Detroit at summer's end, she got an agent and her son and daughter both began working.

Judy was savvy enough to locate and read *Variety* where she saw a casting call for *Mame*. She started writing the producers, sending them pictures of her son. They kept telling her that he was too young.

Finally, her son wrote them a letter himself, sending a tape of his voice and $1 requesting that the producers listen to his tape and use the money for postage to send the tape back if they didn't like it.

Judy received a letter by return mail saying that the producers would see her son when they came to Detroit.

After hearing him sing, the producers gave Mark a script and asked him to read a scene with the star. He had already memorized the show, so when they handed him a script, he was able to set it aside and do the entire scene with the star, touching her so deeply that she cried. He started work the next week.

People in the hinterlands write me every day asking me how they can get started in the business when they don't live in New York, Los Angeles or Chicago. Judy is a perfect example of the entrepreneurial spirit that sees no obstacle. Judy believes that children who are successful in the business have a true calling. Mark was lucky he had a mom who was smart enough to help him realize his dreams.

Don't Get Professional Pictures Right Away

Since young children change so rapidly, children's agents do not expect professional pictures. Once you have an agent, he will want to advise you on your pictures, so at the beginning, a clear snapshot is all that is needed.

Send pictures by snail or electronic mail with a note giving all the vital statistics: age, weight, height, coloring and anything the child might have done involving getting up in front of people and taking direction. Professional experience is not nearly as important as the child being comfortable with people. Happy. Confident. Gregarious.

If the snapshot interests the agent, he will ask you to bring the child in for an interview. You will be invited out while the agent gets a feel for how the child behaves in the same kind of situation that will take place for an audition.

If you are a child reading this, know that agents are very impressed when you make your own arrangements. It means you are motivated, organized and adult. A children's agent told me that her role model for a child actor was a client who at 13 had done lots of local theatre, called Screen Actors Guild, got a list of agents and sent in pictures himself. He got the first job he went for: the national tour of *The Sound of Music*.

Children are paid the same fee per day as adults and will be expected (all things being equal) to behave as adults. No sulking, tantrums or crankiness. They don't like it when adult actors do that either!

Training

Although kids can get jobs by just being cute, outgoing and well behaved, continuing in the business past the 'darling' years demands training.

One of the reasons that those kids that you see on talk shows lamenting that Hollywood deserted them is that in those days the prevailing attitude was, "Don't get them trained. Leave them natural." I was even told that about my own kids (and this was in the 70s), but I looked around and I said, "There's something wrong with this picture, you wouldn't enter any other profession in the world without training." So I started searching for an acting teacher. I had had no training and I didn't even know what I was looking for, but I found Diane Hardin's Joy of Acting and I sat there in tears the whole night long and I said, "This is what I am looking for."

I sent my own kids and later, all my clients. That's one of the reasons that clients that I have raised have been able to make the transition, if they wanted to. A lot of them don't want to. A lot of them go off to college and do something else.

Of the children that I take, if they have the passion, if they get trained, they usually get to work, even if it's only commercials.
– Judy Savage, The Savage Agency Los Angeles

Teachers and coaches for acting, voice and dance for kids and young adults are discussed on page 43-44.

Babies

Show business is the only industry in America in which babies can legally work. Laws governing their employment vary widely from state to state and in general, they are astonishingly lax. California is one of the few to specifically prohibit the employment of prematurely born babies on film and TV productions. In 18 states, there is no regulation or protection at all.
– Deadline.com[31]

Babies are a whole other part of the business. Many children's agents don't deal with infants and babies at all unless the babies are twins or triplets and even then, it is sometimes easier for agents to go through managers.

We rely on managers for babies because babies with a manager require less upkeep. I'll get a baby call and put it out to a manager and they'll send me a list of kids. I can just make one phone call to the manager and say, "Get these kids out." Sometimes calls come in really late and it makes it difficult.

With baby-moms, they are usually so new to the business that you have to do so much explaining about going on interviews and how you go, how you dress and how to get there and then they have a million questions. We're not opposed to answering the questions except when we are really busy.
– Vivian Hollander, HTG/Hollander Talent Group Los Angeles

What Agents Look for in Young Actors
Since there are very strict labor laws in California, in addition to kids who are more interested in acting than T-ball, agents look at specific age groups for pragmatic reasons:

We always need new 6-year-olds, especially 6-year-olds that can play 4, because it means they can work all day. We are also always looking for 18-year-olds who can play 15-16-17. These are the perfect ages to get started. Adult agents have clients that will stay the same for 10-15 years, children change every 6 months: they grow up, they get braces, they don't want to do it, they lose teeth, they want to play T-ball, all kinds of things.
– Judy Savage, The Savage Agency

You have to be 6-years old to work all day and 18 to work without restrictions like having an adult on the set with you and requiring the producers to set aside some portion of the day for your education. In the recent past, more and more television shows market to kids in the 8-12 age range on the Disney Channel, Nickelodeon, Cartoon Network and The Hub. This has led to a big demand for child and teenage actors.

The shows make being famous look appealing, but never deal with the repercussions of all that attention, freedom and scrutiny.

Disney Channel spokeswoman Patti McTeague said the 24-hour media microscope can magnify existing issues for any actor, especially a teenager. "So much of what they say and do, especially in their private lives, is chronicled and transmitted to millions of people and the Internet adds a whole new twist," McTeague said. "Nobody, nobody can live under that spotlight for very long and not have it impact them in some way. Some deal with it differently than others."

Disney, like Nickelodeon, offers a "Talent 101" course that seeks to prepare young talent for the pressure that might lie ahead, such as being recognized while shopping and managing their image online. The Disney course includes a licensed clinical psychologist and addresses privacy concerns, taking care of oneself (physically and emotionally), coping strategies and security issues.
– Los Angeles Times [32]

It's difficult for even adult actors to withstand the "no rules environment" that comes with stardom. Some are able to hold onto themselves and stay normal at first, but with so much adulation and attention, pretty soon they do what human beings are supposed to do, they adapt. And it can be ugly.

"Some of these young actors start to become caught up in the show-business machine," said John Kirby, an acting coach who has worked with young actors on such films as The Chronicles of Narnia: The Lion, the Witch and the Wardrobe *and the* 2003 Peter Pan. *"The visibility is so great that honestly, I'm not surprised that so many of them are having problems."*
– Ibid. [33]

When I've cautioned parents in the past about putting kids and teens in the business, they frequently say, "Oh, but she loves it. She's dying to do it. This is what the wants."

I'm sure she would like to eat ice cream all day too. Her brain is not fully developed yet and she doesn't have the capacity to make an informed decision. It's the job of parents to protect children from themselves. Years ago, a casting director wanted my then-ten-year-old daughter to read for the lead in a movie. I believed then and I believe now that there is no way a ten-year-old plays a lead in the movie and is still a ten-year-old at the end of that process. The movie turned out to be an iconic movie. The young girl who played the lead has pretty much had a trainwreck of a life afterwards. Parents beware.

Set-Sitters

Parents should be prepared to ferry children to auditions and if the child books a job, to be on the set at all times. Not only is it a SAG rule that a parent or designated set-sitter of some type be provided, but it is *never* wise to leave your child in an adult environment on his own.

Someone needs to be your child's advocate. No matter what the job or how good the management, the studio is in the business to make money. Someone must be on set who is not afraid of losing his job if he says that the set is too hot or the kid needs a break. We all want to please and do a good job, but certain rules must be followed.

You or your designated representative should be always with your child. You and your child should know the SAG-AFTRA and Equity rules about school time, rest breaks, overtime and wardrobe fittings.

You don't have to be a member to access the SAG-AFTRA website to check out the helpful information and videos available for kids and parents at sagaftra.org/content/for-parents.

As discussed earlier, having a manager can be helpful at the beginning of a child's career not only being a conduit to a good agent, but educating both parent and child about work permits, audition behavior and other details of the business. While some agents don't mind helping with those things, some say that means they have less time for pitching the client. The mothers' "on set grapevine" does a pretty good job educating themselves and each other, so if you want to forego the manager, the SAG-AFTRA content for kids mentioned above is a good place to start.

It's imperative that parents recognize their role in the process.

"What parents have to understand is, they are the excess baggage that comes along with the talent," says Innovative Artists' Claudia Black. "It's the parents' responsibility to make sure the child is prepared, on time and has rehearsed the scene. "....If agents can't get along with the parent, they won't take the kid. It's really not just about the kid being amazing," says Cunningham Escott Dipene's Alison Newman. "It's a joint thing, fifty-fifty.

— New York Magazine[34]

Parents may be viewed as excess baggage, but they are necessary baggage. If your child begins to work steadily, it's a full time job for one of the parents. It might be exciting at first, but when/if your child is really successful, you might find yourself not only in an inferior position on the set, but also with your child.

Examine your reasons for putting your child under such stress. If your child is motivated and has dreamed of acting forever, that's one thing. If he's just excited about seeing himself on television or if you always wanted to act, but didn't, you should step back and reconsider.

Children
✓ can get by with a snapshot to begin with
✓ are paid as adults, must behave as adults
✓ must be able to talk to anyone
✓ require a set-sitter
✓ are only half the package, it's the parents' job too

Parents
✓ get a full time job if the child starts working, but no respect
✓ should consider all the ramifications of their decision

chapter 16

Researching the Agents

There are various categories of agents and managers: big, small, credible, wannabes, beginning, aggressive, just getting by. Since rep/client relationships are personal, any classifications I make are subjective. I'm presenting the facts as best I can, based upon my research and personal experience both in interviewing these agents and my years in the business. You must digest the information and make your own decisions.

There are new agents building their lists who, like you, will be the stars of tomorrow. You could become a star with the right one-agent office and you could die on the vine at CAA.

There are no guarantees, no matter whom you choose. The most important office in town might sign you even without your union card if your reel and/or resume excites them. But mostly they don't take developmental clients. They want you when you are further along. Whomever you choose, if you are to have a career of longevity, you can never surrender your own vigilance in the process of your career.

Evaluate Carefully

If you read carefully, you'll make a wise decision using client lists, the agents' own words, and the listing of each agency. Don't write anyone off. In this business no one knows anything. I love my agent, but you might hate him.

There are nice people who are good agents and there are nice people who are not. There are people who are not nice who are good agents and so on. Just because I may think some agent is a jerk doesn't mean he is. And if he is, that might make him a good agent. Who knows?

If you read all the listings, you will have an overview. I've endeavored to present the facts, plus whatever might have struck me about the agent: this one was once known as "The Goat Lady", that one was an Equity rep.

Some agents have survived for years without ever really representing their clients. They wait for the phone to ring. Some agents talk a better game than they play. I believe it would be better to have no agent than one who is going to lie to you.

Agent Stereotypes

We all know the stereotypes about agents: they lie, that's their job. While some agents lie, most don't. Most are hard-working, professional, regular people who, like you, want to make it in show business.

Like you, they want to be respected for their work, go to the Academy Awards and get great tables at restaurants. And again, like you, they are willing to put up with the toughest, most heartbreaking business in the world because they are mavericks who love the adventure and can't think of a single thing that interests them more.

Many who read this book are just starting out and will be scanning the listings for people who seem to be building their lists. Many of those agents have great potential. Some don't.

Who's Included in This Book?

Anybody who would talk to me? Only those agents that I could actually in good conscience, recommend? It seems inappropriate for me to try to play God about who is worthy and who is not.

On the other hand, I don't want my readers to think I would recommend everyone who is in the book. That automatically makes anyone not in the book suspect.

When the first edition of this book was published, I only included agencies, other than the conglomerates, whose offices I personally visited and interviewed. These days, in the interests of time and geography, there are more that I have only met on the phone. My updates have been done on the phone. The majority of the profiles are still based on personal contact.

Most of the time I went to the office because that was most convenient for the agent. Seeing the office also helped refine my thinking about the agency. I didn't meet everyone in every agency or all the partners, but I did always meet with a partner or an agent who was acting as a spokesperson for the company. I could be wrong in my judgments, but at least they are not based on hearsay.

Number of Clients

The number of clients listed at the end of an agency profile only refers to theatrical clients, unless otherwise specified. Just as the box office receipts reported in *Variety* might be inflated for business reasons, an agency may under report the size of their list. In reality they may have more clients than they can reasonably represent and they would just as soon not publicize that fact.

As mentioned earlier, the general agent-to-client ratio to look for is at least one agent for every twenty to twenty-five clients. Although a good agent will tell you that's the number to shoot for, it's rare that you get an agency that adheres to that, regardless of the numbers they report.

Realistically, how is an agent going to give personal attention to more than twenty-five clients? And also realistically, unless the clients are on series, how is a small agent to pay his bills with only twenty-five clients?

Most of the profiles in this book list a few clients from the agency's list. Sometimes I looked at IMDbPro and chose some names and sometimes agents gave me some names and sometimes agents objected strongly to my mentioning any names at all, so if you find a profile with no clients listed, just go to IMDbPro yourself and have a look.

Though IMDbPro has a wealth of useful information if you know where to look, their search engine isn't very flexible. If you don't know the exact spelling of a name, even a big celeb name, IMDbPro is not google and may not be able to find what you are looking for. I looked for various agencies that weren't listed, but when I queried the agent's name, magically the listing for the agency appeared.

I happen to know some of their information isn't accurate because I saw agencies listed that I know have been out of business for a while. Even so, enough data is correct that you can draw reasonable conclusions for your purposes.

There are several tabs at IMDbPro: clients, staff, main page, etc. All are interesting and all bear scrutiny. Under the client tab, for instance, note whether the client is an actor, writer, host, musician, commercial actor, etc., and notice that sometimes there are multiple agents listed. Also look carefully at credits. Some of those movies are self-produced shorts. That's not a bad thing, but says more to the entrepreneurial talents of the actor than necessarily the efforts of the agent.

IMDb is free while IMDbPro charges for access. At first, I thought I would only subscribe briefly to IMDbPro, but now I consider my subscription a necessity.

You can get a free two week trial to evaluate the service.

Less Is More

Once you feel you actually have something to interest an agent – a reel, a play in production, and/or some swell reviews from decent venues – be discriminating in your quest for representation.

Don't blanket the town with letters. Target three agents that seem right for you and ration your money, time, and energy. It's more likely to pay off than the scattershot approach.

Agents are already inundated with DVDs and reviews and while they are all looking for the next hot actor, there are only so many hours in a day. Don't waste their time or yours.

If you are just starting, don't set your heart on CAA, choose someone who is at your level so you can grow together.

A job is not automatic agent entrée. As noted throughout this book, most agents are not interested in a one shot deal.

Don't despair. Agents agree that new blood is what keeps the industry going. Even if you have thirty pairs of shoes and swear you will never buy another, if you see shoes that captivate you, you will buy them. The trick is to be captivating, or more importantly, marketable.

Like attracts like. You will ultimately get just what you want in an agent if you take the time to discover what that is. I believe you can get a terrific agent if you become a terrific client. There are no shortcuts. And today is not the last day of your life.

In her book, *My Lives*, Roseanne quotes a line from Sun Tzu's *The*

Art of War, which she says everyone in Hollywood has read. It basically says: "The one who cares most, wins."

Kevin Bacon/Referrals

As you read the agency listings, you will see that many of the agents, though they will look at submissions, are not open to being contacted by new people who have no one in the industry to recommend them.

If you don't know anyone, remember "The Kevin Bacon Game." It's the same concept as the play/movie *Six Degrees of Separation*, which contends that anyone in the world can find an association with anyone else in the world through six associations: in "The Kevin Bacon Game" it only takes three degrees, and in some cases, less.

It goes like this. Your mother shops at the same grocery store as Kevin Bacon, or in my own case, I have worked with Kyra Sedgewick who is married to Kevin Bacon. Ostensibly, if I had a script I wanted to get to Kevin, I ought to be able to get it to him through Kyra.

If you track all the odds and ends of your life, you should be able to produce somebody who knows somebody who knows somebody who can make an authentic (however tenuous) connection to someone who can make a call for you. Otherwise you are just querying/calling cold.

If you can't come up with a connection, write the best darn letter in the world and knock some agent on his butt. However, if you can score at "The Kevin Bacon Game," it would be best.

Remember

✓ Your first agent is yourself. You must be your own agent until you attract someone who will care and has more access than you. It's better to keep on being your own agent than to have an agent without access or passion.

✓ Make yourself read all the listings before you make a decision.

✓ Mass mailings are a waste of money. There is no use sending WME or CAA a letter without entrée. It's pointless to query someone you have never heard of. If you have no information about the agent, how do you know you want him? Take the long view. Look for an agent you would want to be with for years. Be selective.

✓ Don't blow your chances of being taken seriously by pursuing an agent before you are ready.

✓ Although rules were made to be broken, presuming on an agent's time by showing up at his office without an appointment or calling to speak to the agent as though you are an old friend, will ultimately backfire. Observe good manners and be sensitive to other people's space and time.

✓ Getting the right agent is not the answer to all your prayers, but it's a start!

✓ Call the agency and confirm the address before you send anything. Things change quickly. The agency won't know it's you.

chapter _17

Agency Profiles

9Muse

356 Broadway, #2
New York, NY 10013
1-646-801-6873
9muse.org

Michael Imbimbo, with his undergraduate degree in Vocal Performance from McGill University in Montreal and his graduate degree from San Francisco Conservatory of Music arrived in New York ready to pursue his career. Immediately struck by how hard it was for young performers to actually translate all those expensive years of study into a living wage, he became interested in artist management.

He began to explore the world of job getting and keeping and got a job at IMG Artists to begin to figure it out. One of Michael's greatest assets is his ability to communicate both in person and via his tech skills. Those skills made Michael valuable at IMG and are one of his most valuable assets as an agent. He has the ability to put his client's web, film and television work in the hands of the buyers almost as soon as it appears.

Though IMDbPro lists 9Muse with only 2 clients, his webpage features many more. You'll see news about Josh Canfeld (*Survivor*, *Natasha, Pierre and the Great Comet of 1812*), Lulu Lloyd (*School of Rock*), Rachel Zatcoff (*Phantom of the Opera*) and other clients listed there.

Michael prefers electronic submissions that include (along with your headshot and resume) a short note about why you are looking for an agent. Michael reviews every submission, but only contacts you if he needs more information. He has no problem with your sending a submission every 3-6 months with your newest credits.

9Muse's website includes a great article under the news tab about getting an agent that I highly recommend.

Agent: Michael Imbimbo
Clients: 60

About Artists Agency

1650 Broadway, #1406
New York, NY 10019
1-212-581-1857
aboutartistsagency.com

Renee Glicker majored in both art and theatre at the State University of New York. Told that if you could be happy doing anything other acting, you should, she tried audience development in Florida and realized that she had to act. Returning to New York, she scored a national tour of *They're Playing Our Song* followed by commercials, cabaret, television, films and off-Broadway.

Her day job at night as a waitress at The Comic Strip allowed her to observe the developing careers of Adam Sandler, Wanda Sykes, Jerry Seinfield, Chris Rock and others. She absorbed so much of their process that up-and-coming comics asked her to critique their work. Club booker Lucien Hold (who became her mentor) noticed and asked Renee to help open a management company for comics.

When Renee heard that a big theatrical agency wanted to create a comedy department, she arrived with her clients and began booking immediately. Three years later, she opened her own agency. Celebrating her 17th anniversary in 2011, Renee reflected on her track record. She booked more actors on *The Sopranos* than any other agent in New York and has actors working as much in film and on television as in theatre.

Clients include Robert Prescott (*Michael Clayton*), Emilio Del Gado (*Sesame Street*), Phyre Hawkins (*Book of Mormon*), Trisha Jeffrey (*Sister Act*), Kevin Duda (*Book of Mormon*), Richard Crawford (*War Horse*), Johnnie Mae (*Boardwalk Empire*) and Allison Semmes (*Book of Mormon*).

Agent: Renee Glicker
Client List: 88 plus freelance

About Face Talent

419 Park Avenue S, #607
New York, NY 10016
1-212-221-1518
no website

Originally established in '02 as Carson Kolker's model & print division, when the Pretties began amassing their own film, theatre and television credentials, that division and those clients became About Face, now led by Alice Skiba.

Obsessed with movies from an early age, Alice knew she wanted to be in the business in some way, but where? She tried acting classes and interning in various talent and casting agencies before realizing that agenting was her path.

Her first job in '04 out of Boston University in '04 was as Barry Kolker's assistant. She began heading up About Face in September 2013. She's joined by junior agent Abby Berger.

Their list of clients include Jamie Clayton, Trace Lysette, Patricia Squire, Victgoria Dicce and Lisann Valentin. They only book principal roles. Check IMDbPro for more information.

Agents: Alice Skiba and Abby Berger
Client List: 25

Abrams Artists Agency

275 7th Avenue
New York, NY 10001
1-646-486-4600
abramsartists.com

Through resourcefulness, determination and an eye for talented agents and artists, Harry Abrams has headed or partnered a string of agencies over the years starting in the 60s with the commercial powerhouse Abrams-Rubaloff and evolving into the powerful and respected theatrical and literary office that is the Abrams Artists Agency of today.

Abrams runs the motion picture and television departments in Los Angeles and leaves the New York office in the hands of vice-president and managing director Robert Attermann and senior VP Neal Altman. Victoria Kress and Jamie Pillet shepherd the youth theatrical clients. The full list of agents is listed below.

Names from their respected theatrical list include Ryan Farrell (*Trainwreck*), Fred Melamed (*Lady Dynamite*), Kelly Bishop (*Bunheads*), Mark Margolis (*My Big Fat Greek Wedding 2*), Judith Ivey (*A Bird of the Air*), Ron Leibman (*The Sopranos*) and others. AAA also handles children and young adults. Clients come to this agency through referral.

Agents: Robert Attermann, Neal Altman, Tracy Weiss, Danielle DeLawder, Genine Esposito, Richard Fisher, Peter Hagan, Amy Mazur, Paul Reisman, Samantha Stoller, Bonnie Shumofsky, Maura Teitelbaum, Mark Turner, Victoria Kress and Jamie Pillet
Client List: 2073 for both coast includes all clients, not just actors

Across the Board Talent

1515 Broadway
New York, NY 10036
1-917-397-0282
atbtalent.com

A driven child actor until age 19, Guy Kochiani abandoned acting for new horizons. While in law school, he worked at various talent agencies, at Universal Records and at a Beverly Hills law firm, and soon established his own production company (JRE) and his own talent agency (The Kochiani Agency). He changed the name to reflect the service he provides and also because casting directors could neither remember, spell or pronounce his last name.

Todd Eskin graduated from the University of Central Florida with a BFA in Musical Theatre Performance and came to New York to pursue his dream. He slowly began to realize that he didn't really have the drive needed for an acting career and began directing, stage managing and doing choreography. That's when he realized how much he enjoyed the helping people side of the business and when he started training to be an agent at Abrams Artists.

VP of Talent, he created the theatre department at ABT. Todd handles theatre bookings while Guy handles television and film. ATB represents actors, directors, screenwriters, models, choreographers, hosts and producers in Los Angeles, New York and Las Vegas.

Their client list includes Ashley Eckstein (*Star Wars: The Clone Wars*), Martin Kove (*The Karate Kid, Cagney & Lacey*), Shelley Regner (*Pitch Perfect*), Jenny Lin (*Best Night Ever*) and Susan Diol (*One Life to Live*). I love this agency: Todd told me that they respond to every submission either with a "yes", come in or "thank you very much." They prefer hard copy submissions.

Agents: Guy Kochiani and Todd Eskin
Clients: 216 (entire list)

Affinity Artists Agency

67 West St. 4th Fl., #32
Brooklyn, NY 11222
1-212-390-1221
affinityartists.com

In hopes of being the next Spielberg, Ross Grossman went to UCLA film school. After graduation, his desire for a schedule and a paycheck intervened, so he moved to San Francisco for a Masters in Clinical Psychology where he started doing stand-up. At one point it was therapy by day, stand-up by night.

Ross was a good shrink, but that wasn't his calling. He moved to NYC where his sister was a manager, to learn that side of the business and returned to San Francisco where he established a successful modeling agency. Still the pull to LA and a more traditional talent agency lingered. He moved to LA, briefly working for Harry Abrams before starting Affinity. That was 2001.

Ross became bicoastal. His New York office is run by the woman who taught him the ropes in the first place, his sister, Lynne. Lynne's early career was as a successful print model. She became a booking agent in Chicago before creating her own modeling agency here in New York. When she sold her agency to a larger agency, she continued there as Agency Director for 16 years until joining Ross in 2010. Clients from their NY list include: Dan Hodapp (*Vinyl*), Jacob Salas (*Orange is the New Black*), Pat Shay *(The Blacklist)* and Sarah Skeist (*Bastards*).

Agent: Lynne Grossman
Clients: 90

APA/Agency for the Performing Arts

135 W 50th St. 17th floor

New York City, NY 10020

1-212-205-4320

apa-agency.com

Founded in the 1960s by expatriates of MCA and ICM, APA is the fourth largest of the corporate agencies with offices in New York, Los Angeles and Nashville. APA represents artists and performers across all media platforms including feature film, television, music, theatre, publishing and digital. They package movies and television series (*Hell on Wheels, 24, Carnivale*, etc.) and represent luxury and lifestyle brands including The Kardashians, Marriott and Lamborghini.

President and CEO Jim Gosnell heads up the talent division and joins his many colleagues representing their clients from New York, Los Angeles and Nashville.

Though APA has prestigious clients in all areas, the stars here are in comedy: Amy Schumer, Kevin Hart, Larry Wilmore, Joy Behar, Louie C. K., Eddie Izzard, etc. Check their website for the whole amazing list: apa-agency.com/comedy. Respected acting clients include Uzo Aduba, Treat Williams and Will Patton.

One reason for the strong comedy presence is that APA is also known as the place for comedy development. They hold regular showcases to introduce clients to buyers.

The diverse Speakers list includes 50 Cent, Al Pacino, Jane Fonda and Arnold Schwarzenegger. The Concert Division sports Poison, Judas Priest, Brian Wilson, Dolly Parton, Run DMC, Broken Lizard and Fleetwood Mac in a complete menu of jazz, contemporary, electronic, country, international and special attractions.

Agents: Jim Gosnell, Mike Berkowitz, Lee Dintsman, etc.
Client List: 2002 ish

Andreadis Talent Agency, Inc.

119 W 57th Street, #711
New York, NY 10019
1-212-315-0303
no website

I'm sorry to report that Barbara Andreadis died unexpectedly in December 2015. Barbara's children now own the agency, but the day to day operation remains much the same as longtime assistants Yvette Rovira and Alexander Stine stepped up to continue Barbara's work.

Tampa native Yvette graduated from Boston's Berklee College of Music where she studied Music Business Management in addition to singing. Andreadis was her first NY job and she moved quickly from intern to assistant to indispensable. In addition to a successful music career (check Youtube), songs on television (*Bones*) and VH1, Yvette's heart is still with her clients and she is now a franchised agent.

Actor, producer, coach Alexander Stine came to the City in 2006 after studying theatre at the University of Northern Colorado. He quickly connected with other UNC theatre grads and alums and lived the actor's life, producing and acting in off-Broadway projects for unlivable wages, waiting tables while demonstrating a talent for connecting fellow actors with jobs. When he was fired from his waiter-job at a fancy restaurant, he decided he wanted a fulfilling day job. His manager put him in touch with Barbara where (also continuing his successful acting career), he followed the same path as Yvette, intern/assistant/indispensable. They both became part of Barbara's family and now that Barbara is gone, they carry her legacy.

Clients include Jeff Lima (*Show Me a Hero*, *Chicago Fire*), Karen Lynn Gorney (*Saturday Night Fever*), Big Daddy Kane *(Exposed)*, Dan Grimaldi (*The Sopranos*) and Beau Baxter (*Hand to God*, B'way).

Agents: Yvette Rovira and Alexander Stine
Client List: 134

Ann Wright Representatives

165 W 46th Street, 10th Floor
New York, NY 10036
1-212-764-6770

When Ann Wright came to New York after training as an actress at prestigious Boston University, she joined the casting pool at CBS. Like many other actors who have an opportunity to explore other areas of the business, she realized there were other ways to use her creative skills and became the assistant to legendary William Morris agent Milton Goldman.

Ann cast commercials at an advertising agency and then worked for both Charles Tranum and Bret Adams before opening her own commercial talent agency in 1964.

Still thought of first as a voiceover and commercial talent agency, the legit department continues to thrive with clients working in theatre, film and television.

Daughter Susan was a trade show producer before running Ann's west coast office for eight years. Back in New York now, she has created a successful youth division for both legit and commercials.

AWR's theatrical list includes Gino Conforte (*Angels & Demons*), Stella Stark (*Law & Order: SVU*), Alice Litvak (*The Americans*) and Oakes Fegley (*Pete's Dragon*).

Agents: Susan Wright and Ann Wright
Client List: 35

Ann Steele Agency

330 W 42nd Street, #1802
New York, NY 10036
1-212-629-9112
no website

Houston native Ann Steele taught at Kansas State Teachers College and at a community college in Illinois, was a Girl Scout Executive in Georgia and the Director of the Girl Scouts for the Borough of Queens before showbiz entered her brain via her son's involvement in a program called Acting by Children.

When Ann started raising money for the group, she observed managers checking out kids, picking choice clients and recognized a ripe business opportunity. She and a partner started their own business representing young actors like Jason Alexander, Michael E. Knight, Kevin Kilner, Alex Winter and Christopher Steele.

Ann retired from managing long ago to agent an impressive list. Some of them are Joel Bernstein (*Mozart in the Jungle*), Tony Naumovski (*Run All Night*), Gene Jones (*The Hateful 8, The Sacrament, No Country for Old Men*) and Nick Abeel (*There Are No Second takes in Life*).

Ann's office is actor friendly with clients in the neighborhood calling to ask if they can bring her a nice coffee. And how can you not love an agent who is known in some circles as Ragtime Ann?

Agent: Ann Steele
Client List: 9

The Artists Group
1650 Broadway, #1105
New York, NY 10019
1-212-586-1452
no website

Originally an actor, Robert Malcolm never intended to be an agent, but in 1984 when his agent Peggy Grant offered him a job with time off for auditions whenever he needed it, he agreed to work for her. Peggy died a few months later and left the agency to Robert and he has not been to an audition since.

Robert's agency has been known as PGA, The Artists Group, The Artists Group East (to distinguish it from the LA office), but now that Robert is no longer bi-coastal, it's just The Artists Goup.

Today, Robert mostly reps an impressive list of longtime clients including Loretta Switt, Nancy Dussault, Tony Lo Bianco, Judy Kaye, Jamie Farr, Carole Cook and Tammy Grimes.

Though committed to his longtime family of actors, Robert is always looking for hot new talent and recently found and signed Ben Chavez, so you never know.

Agent: Robert Malcolm
Client List: 18

Atlas Talent

15 E 32nd Street, 6th fl.

New York, NY 10016

1-212-730-4500

atlastalent.com

In 2000 Lisa Marber-Rich, Jonn Wasser, John Hossenlopp and Ian Lesser left Don Buchwald & Associates to create a broadcast agency providing talent for on camera and voiceover commercials, promotionals, narrations, documentaries, trailers, audio books and animation.

Prior to their Buchwald stints, Lisa was an Account Manager in advertising at Bates, DMB&B, and Foote Cone Belding, Ian Lesser was in film production at Tribeca Studio and Jonn Wasser was in marketing at Radio City and worked as a freelance entertainment writer with articles published in *Details* and other national magazines.

With today's technology, it's easy to voice a New York job while in Los Angeles, or anyplace else in the world, so Atlas sports an impressive international list that includes Lori Petty, Robert Englund, Barry Bostwick, Lily Tomlin, Frank Langella and Kathy Bates as well as their list of anonymous celebrity voices that reside all over the world.

These days, John Wasser splits his time between the New York and Los Angeles offices.

Agents: Lisa Marber-Rich, Jonn Wasser, John Hossenlopp, Zoe Yellen, Mackenzie Samet, Ricky Meyer and Ian J. Fisher

Client List: 422 VO and on camera

Avalon Artists Group

242 W 30th St., #903
New York City, NY 10001
1-212-868-3200
avalonaratists.com

When he was 12 years old, Craig Holtzberg told his parents he wanted to be an actor. They said he could do whatever he wanted to do as soon as he graduated business school. So the day after he graduated from the University of Colorado at Boulder, Craig moved to Los Angeles to become an actor. Soon though, Craig changed direction, working in retail and fashion and moving to NY to take a job as Senior Vice-President of Sales and Marketing for Calvin Klein. When the business downsized and Craig was contemplating options, a friend told Craig that his agent had an opening for an agent.

His first reaction was, "That's not something I ever thought of." His friend said, "You were an actor, you have a business degree, you love theatre, who could be a better agent than you?".

He took the meeting and was hired by Patty Woo at HWA as a commercial agent quickly segueing into legit as well. By 2005, he moved back to Los Angeles and opened his bicoastal agency, joined by all his loyal clients.

Colleague Bernadette McBrinn was also an actor. She joined Craig in 2010 as an intern and quickly became an assistant and then agent in the kids commercials department. Today, she works alongside Craig in the adult legit department. Michelle Thompson heads the youth department repping kids for theatrical as well as commercials.

Clients from their list include Annie Funke (*Criminal Minds: Beyond Borders, Wicked*), Alison Luff (*Matilda: the Musical*), Danny Gardner (*Dames at Sea*) and Brittany Johnson (*Beautiful*).

Agents: Craig Holtzberg, Bernadette McBrinn and Michelle Thompson
Clients: 168 (both coasts)

BRS/Gage Talent Agency

1650 Broadway, #1410
New York, NY 10019
1- 212-757-0098
brsgage.com

Bauman, Redanty & Shaul and The Gage Goup merged their talents in 2014 creating a synergy that has benefitted both the agencies and their clients combining the respected agents of both offices on both coasts into a stronger team to nurture the clients of both.

New York partner Mark Redanty's first job after studying acting and directing at Ithaca College was as a trainee at Raglyn-Shamsky Agency where he became a franchised agent. He worked for Richard Astor before joining (then) Bauman-Hiller in 1984.

Phil Adelman was an elementary school teacher, quiz show writer, director, screenwriter, director of musicals and a composer-lyricist before changing sides of the desk at The Gage Group 30 years ago. Theatre major Steve Unger was an English teacher in New Jersey who really wanted to work in casting or at an agency. He knew the name of every actor in every show. His cousin worked in casting and told him there was an opening at The Gage Group. 15 minutes into his interview, he was hired. That was 35 years ago. Steve says it seems like yesterday! Charles Bodner began his career with Peter Strain before joining BRS.

Clients from their list include Tovah Feldshuh, Annette O'Toole, Danny Burstein, Debra Monk, Billy Magnussen, Richard Lewis, Dennis Christopher and Michael Nouri. BRS only works with signed clients.

Partners David Shaul and Martin Gage run the Los Angeles office.

Agents: Mark Redanty, Phil Adelman, Steve Unger, Charles Bodner, Erika Karnell and Sarabeth Schedeen
Client List: 562

bloc

630 Ninth Avenue, # 702
New York, NY 10036
1-212-924-6200
nyc.blocagency.com

Canadian brother and sister Laney and Brendan Filuks moved to Los Angeles with no thought of ever being in the agency business: Laney left home to dance and act; Brendan to work for SONY. But as Laney became the go-to person whenever her agent, Dorothy Day Otis, needed help with the dance clients, she and Brendan hit upon the idea to open an agency with a focus solely on dancers. After all, their mother had her own dance studio, so they knew about dancers.

Bloc means people coming together for a common goal. Though listed as Bloc Talent Agency at IMDb, the Filuks like to think of themselves as bloc. So says the logo on their webpage. They rep actors, singers, choreographers and extreme athletes for legit, film, television and print in New York, Los Angeles and Atlanta.

Fatima Wilson, Jim Daly, Maegan Mishico and Emily Watson collectively run the New York office servicing clients ages 18 and up for film, legit, television and commercials.

If you submit to this agency online, do not mail information directly to a particular agent as that mail is regarded as spam. Use only their submission page. If you use snail mail, include a cover letter with any referrals you might have. Include performance links. Bloc holds general auditions annually; check the webpage for particulars.

Adair Wellington, AJ Blankenship, Alex Grayson, Alsson Solomon, Barry Busby, Ben Cherry, Donald Jones, Jr. and Martina Sykes are names from their list. You can find out everything about the agency and who just booked what at their excellent website nycblocagency.com.

Agents: Fatima Wilson, Jim Daly, Maegan Mishico and Emily Watson
Client List: 128

Bret Adams Agency

448 W 44th Street
New York, NY 10036
1-212-765-5630
bretadamsltd.net

When actress Margi Roundtree graduated from the American Academy of Dramatic Arts, she became Company Manager for a respected off-off Broadway theatre. When the theatre folded, she was eager to finally pursue her acting career and loathe to accept the plea of a friend to be BAA's front desk person. It's 30 years later and Margi's now one of the owners playing a leading part every day in the careers of her clients.

About to get his degree in acting at NYU, Ken Malamed was nervous about auditioning, so he interviewed for a casting internship at Playwrights Horizons. After that, he refocused his sights from acting to casting or agenting, alternating between both while still writing. Finally he took off five years to write, but had to come back because he missed agenting so much. He agented briefly with Honey Sanders before joining the BAA family and ultimately becoming a partner.

Northwestern grad Bruce Ostler co-founded a Chicago improv group, created, pitched, produced and wrote for theatre, television and films before the uncertainty of the business got to him. He joined BAA as an assistant, became an agent at Fifi Oscard and returned to BAA as a partner when Bret Adams offered him a partnership and an opportunity to create the literary department.

Bret created this agency in 1977. When he retired, Bruce, Margi and Ken bought the agency. BAA has a literary department handling writers, directors, designers and composers. BAA's website is amazing. A co-venture with their clients, it features pictures, resumes and links.

Agents: Bruce Ostler, Margi Roundtree, Ken Melamed, Mark Orsini and Alexis Williams
Client List: 180

CAA/Creative Artists Agency

405 Lexington Avenue, 19th Floor
New York, NY 10174
1-212-277-9000
caa.com

Ask.com agrees with practically everyone else on the planet: "CAA is considered the largest and most powerful talent agency in the world, and Richard Lovett runs it. At 41 years old, he took over as head of CAA in 1995 after starting in its mail room right after college. Lovett has had a hand in the careers of nearly everyone involved with today's blockbusters."

All you have to do is visit their IMDbPro page to begin salivating at the names on the list: Will Smith, Bradley Cooper, Emily Blunt, Scarlett Johansson, Brad Pitt, Ann Hathaway, Lee Pace, Robert De Niro, Matthew McConaughey, Chris Pine, Meryl Streep, Eddie Redmayne and on and on.

WME, UTA and ICM may be nipping ferociously at their heels, but so far, not even counting the 2015 March revolt of ten agents leaving in the dead of night with a worrisome list of comedy talent, nothing has managed to dim CAA's light.

CAA not only has offices in the places you might expect – New York, Los Angeles, Nashville, Chicago, London – but has a presence in Beijing, Stockholm, Munich, Switzerland and Mumbai.

IMDbPro says CAA has a staff of 278 and 3294 clients. That's about one agent for every 11.8 clients. I doubt that time considerations break down that way, so if you're not Tom Hanks or Meryl Streep, you might not get as much attention as they, but still, having CAA say your name would still be worth a lot.

Agents: Richard Lovett and 277 others
Client List: 3294

Carlton, Goddard & Freer Talent

352 7th Avenue, #1601
New York, NY 10001
1-212-520-1023
cgft.com

All successful performers, Joel Carlton, Michael Goddard and Christopher Freer never worked together as actors, but as agents they bonded as competitive colleagues with shared goals and style. That synergy produced this agency in January 2012.

Michael Goddard's extreme marketing skills from Arizona State University led to jobs not only for himself and for his actor friends, so after checking Broadway, National Tours and Regional Theatre off his to-do list, he went with marketing and finished his last showbiz job one day and started work at Nicolosi & Co. the next. That was in 2006.

Long Island native Christopher Freer traded in his dancing shoes to become an agent for DDO and KSA in Los Angeles in 2000. Three years later, he headed to New York to create and head the New York office of Clear Talent where he stayed for the next eight years.

Joel Carlton's BFA from Webster University not only prepared him for 14 years as an actor, but served him well as a casting director and an Equity business rep before he began his agenting career with The Luedtke Agency. He spent four years with DGRW and two at Jeanne Nicolosi before joining with Christopher and Michael.

Clients include Noah Racey (*Curtains, Never Gonna Dance*), Hunter Ryan Herdlicka (*A Little Night Music*), Megan McGinnis (*Les Miz*), Dominic Colon (*Southpaw*), T.J. Kenneally (*Blood Ties*), Stephanie Umoh (*Ragtime*), Will Blum (*Book of Mormon*), Lindsay Mendez (*Wicked, Dogfight*), Nathan Lee Graham (*Zoolander 2*), Felicia Boswell (*Shuffle along, Motown*) and Judy McLane (*Momma Mia*)

Agents: Joel Carlton, Michael Goddard and Christopher Freer
Client List: 68

Carry Company

20 W 20th Street, 2th floor
New York, NY 10011
1-212-768-2793
carrycompany.com

Sharon Carry was working at a sports bar in 1990 when she got the idea to send out her well known patrons on the commercial auditions she read about in the trades.

She grew that business to include actors and athletes across the board and now has clients working in film, television and on Broadway.

Carry has so many clients working in Los Angeles that in 2005 she opened the west coast office. She divides her time between the coasts and says she has a terrific assistant in each office.

Don't postcard this agency unless you have something real to say. "Hello, how are you?" doesn't count. They prefer flyers when you are doing something. Sharon says she takes flyers and work very seriously.

In business now for 25 years, Sharon says she really isn't looking for clients right now and when she is, it's industry referral only.

She asked me not to name clients, so you'll have to check IMDbPro. Sharon prefers snail mail.

Agent: Sharon Carry
Client List: 38

Carson-Adler Agency, Inc.

250 W 57th Street #2030
New York, NY 10107
1-212-307-1882
carsonadler.com

As a showbiz mom, Nancy Carson viewed a side of the business that inspired her to start an agency where children would be protected. She trained with children's agency Jan J. before joining with the late Marion Adler to form C-A in 1982. Daughter Bonnie Deroski finally grew tired of rejection and is Nancy's colleague along with Shirley Faison. Her background in management at the National Black Theatre and as another showbiz mom makes Shirley another perfect advocate.

Carson Adler's roster includes Rachel Hilson (*The Good Wife*), Julianna Rose Mauriello *(Lazy Town)*, Andrew Keenan-Bolger, Andy Richardson, Jess LeProtto (all in *Newsies*), MacKenzie Mauzy, Matthew Gumley, Emma Rayne Lyle, Eric Nelsen, Cruz Santiago, Remy Zaken, David DeVries, Ben Liebert, Kiril Kulish, Frankie Galasso & Nathan Scherich *(Jersey Boys)*, Imani Smith (*Lion King*), Eden Duncan-Smith, Zach Rand, Andy Jones, Eamon Foley, Madeline Taylor, Ken Barnett (*February House*), Luke Mannikus, Issadora Tulalian, Lara Teeter, Tyler Merna, Kara Oates (*Mary Poppins, 30 Rock*), Anthony Festa and Sam Poon.

Nancy's keen eye for kids with talent spotted Britney Spears, Ben Affleck, Matt Damon, Lea Michele, Donald Faison, Cynthia Nixon and repped them all when they were still under 18.

Nancy's book *Raising a Star* is a must read for any parent planning to take the journey and Nancy's website is a treasure house of resources for parent and performer.

Agents: Nancy Carson, Bonnie Deroski and Shirley Faison
Client List: 108

Carson Kolker Organization

18 E 41st Street, #801
New York, NY 10017
1-212-221-1517
no website

Created in 1992 by Steve Carson and wife Maria Burton-Carson, CKO was known as The Carson Organization, but in 2004 when Carson retired and sold the agency to colleague Barry Kolker (Henderson Hogan, Fifi Oscard), the name morphed into Carson Kolker quietly reflecting both history and the present.

The agency's family approach provides nurturing as well as opportunity and is a good choice for actors of all ages looking for a home. Although casting directors think of them as one of the first places to go for infants, twins and children, CKO welcomes all age groups.

Clients include Hadley DeLany (*Louie*), Lonette McKee (*Malcolm X*), Kurt McKinney (*General Hospital*), Kristen Alderson (*One Life to Live*), Robert Hallak (*Veronica Mars*), Ilene Kristen (*One Life to Live*), Eddie Alderson (*One Life to Live, Reservation Road*), Georgi James (*Annie, Billy Elliot*) Gaten Matarazzo (*Stranger Things*), Ed Heavey (*Outsiders*) and James DePaiva (*One Life to Live*).

Barry looks at all pictures and resumes seriously and says that he has found clients from the mail. The legit department does not freelance, while the print and commercial department will freelance with the intent to sign.

Though they have similar names, Carson Kolker is no relation to Carson-Adler.

Agents: Barry Kolker and Alice Skiba
Client List: 90

Clear Talent Group

325 West 38th St., # 1203
New York, NY 10018
1-212- 840-4100
cleartalentgroup.com

New York CTG director Jamie Harris joined Clear at its birth in 2003 and now heads the NY office. His list of dance credits ranges from Radio City Music Hall to Broadway to the Silver Screen.

When Jamie moved to New York, his background helped him book clients on *Law & Order: SVU, Blue Bloods, Louie, Boardwalk Empire, One Life to Live, Nurse Jackie, Good Wife and Gossip Girl, PAN AM, Person of Interest, Royal Pains, White Collar* and in numerous feature films.

This agency also represents directors, writers, artistic directors, choreographers, set designers and lighting designers. Their development department works with clients developing their theatre, television, film and reality television projects and live shows.

Colleagues Chase Renouf and Justin Busch (Phoenix Artists) join Jamie repping Jack Harding and Courtney Galiano (*Glee*), Chauna Bloom (*American Horror Story*), Brooklyn McLinn (*Rules of Engagement*), Rico Rodriguez (*Modern Family*), Logan Browning (*Meet the Browns*), Erica Mansfield (*How to Succeed in Business without Really Trying*) and Ayo Jackson (*Spiderman: Turn off the Dark*) and the rest of their terrific list.

Agents: Jamie Harris, Chase Renouf, Juliana Lichtman and Justin Busch
Client List: 626

Cornerstone Talent Agency

37 W 20th Street, 1007
New York, NY 10011
1-212-807-8344
no website

Though he was planning to use his 1991 history degree from the University of Wisconsin to become a lawyer, Steve Stone started training to be a general manager at Niko Associates the minute he graduated. He did that in tandem with being concessions manager eight shows a week at Tony Randall's National Actor's Theatre. In 1993 he was hired as assistant to Bob Duva (The Gersh Agency, Duva-Flack). When Duva left, he took Steve along as an assistant. A year later Steve was franchised as an agent. He created Cornerstone in September 1997.

Mark Schlegel (APA, Ambrosio/Mortimer, J. Michael Bloom, APA) planned to be a banker but when he landed a gofer job for Mitch Leigh working on *The King and I* as part of his communications major at Indiana's DePauw University, banking didn't stand a chance. His background somewhat mirrors Steve's since both began working for producers and also worked with/for Robbie Lantz.

CTA's list includes Sara Ramirez (*Spamalot*), Daniel Sunjata (*Graceland*), Jon Michael Hill (*Elementary*), Anna Belknap (*CSI: New York*), Jefferson Mays (*A Gentleman's Guide*), Bryce Pinkham (*A Gentleman's Guide*), Carole Shelley (*Billy Elliot*), Lois Smith (*True Blood*), Lillias White (*Fela*), Terrence Mann (*Tiffany*), Jayne Atkinson (*House of Cards*), Isiah Whitlock, Jr. (*The Wire*), Gretchen Egolf (*Journeyman*), Edward Hibbert (*Curtains*), David Garrison (*Married with Children*), Katie Rose Clarke (*Allegiance*), Ana Reeder (*Damages*), Joel de la Fuente (*Man in the High Castle*), Darren Goldstein (*The Affair*), Damian Young (*House of Cards*) and Harry Ford (*Code Black*).

Agents: Steve Stone and Mark Schlegel
Client List: 75

DDO Artists Agency

175 Varick St, #268
New York, NY 10014
1-212-379-6314
ddoagency.com

DDO's roots go back to 1969 in Los Angeles when Dorothy Day Otis created a top children's agency representing the kids from many hit shows including both *The Brady Bunch* and *Different Strokes*. Today DDO is a full service agency repping artists in every medium with offices in New York, Las Vegas, Nashville and Miami.

Bill Bohl and Abby Girvin worked for DDO in Los Angeles for years before purchasing the agency in 1995. Marlene Sutton (Sutton Barth Vennari) became their partner in 1996. At that point Bill created one of the first dance departments in LA, while Marlene joined with Maria Walker to build their successful commercial department.

Jerry Kallarakkal heads up the New York office. Colleagues Irene Cabrera and Gina Manfredi (who heads the Kids Department) help him rep their actors, singers and dancers for film, television, Broadway, off-Broadway, resident productions and national and international tours.

Clients include Kit Treece (*A Chorus Line*), Jake Choi (*Younger*), Craig Geraghty (*Death Pact*) and J.W. Cortes (*Gotham*).

DDO maintains offices in New York, Los Angeles, Las Vegas and Nashville. This agency opens all mail and is constantly looking to fill in gaps. The client list number below is my best guest for theatrical clients based on IMDbPro listing not including commercial clients.

Agents: Jerry Kallarakkal, Irene Cabrera and Gina Manfredi
Client List: 80

DGRW/Douglas, Gorman, Rothacker & Wilhelm

33 W 46th Street, #801
New York, NY 10036
1-212-382-2000
no website

Barry Douglas, Fred Gorman, Flo Rothacker and Jim Wilhelm created DGRW in 1988. Jim Wilhelm is now the sole remaining partner. An actor at fifteen, he was a stage manager, a PR director, a general manager and a casting director before becoming franchised in 1981. Jim is joined by three diverse colleagues.

Psychology major Josh Pultz arrived from upstate New York in 1998 and began interning at DGRW within a week of graduation. Thinking he wanted to be a general manager, he left to work with producer Cameron Macintosh and general manager Alan Wasser but he missed DGRW and returned to become a franchised agent.

An actress when she interned at DGRW in 2005, Nicole Wichinsky now uses her Communications/Film Business and Theatre degrees from the University of Miami repping clients.

Names from the hundred or so actors on DGRW's list include Daniel Dae Kim (*Lost*), Kathleen Chalfant (*Wit*), Elaine Page (*Cats, Evita*), Cybill Shepherd (*The L Word*), Alice Ripley (*Next to Normal*), Patrick Page (*Spiderman*), Montego Glover (*Memphis*), Paige O'Hara (*Les Misérables*), Lynn Cohen (*Munich*), Harry Groener *(Crazy for You)*, Ron Raines *(The Guiding Light)* and Alan Campbell (*Jake and the Fatman*).

DGRW also represents directors, fight directors, choreographers, and musical directors. In addition to agenting, Jim teaches master classes at the University of Cincinnati/College Conservatory of Music.

Agents: Jim Wilhelm, Josh Pultz and Nicole Wichinsky
Client List: 80

Don Buchwald & Associates
10 E 44th Street

New York, NY 10017

1-212-867-1070

buchwald.com

Former actor and producer Don Buchwald (Monty Silver, Abrams-Rubaloff) created the agency in 1977. DBA covers the spectrum of entertainment representation with divisions for film, theatre, television, broadcast, commercial, literary, packaging, syndication, personal appearances and youth.

Although DB&A has visible clients (Ralph Macchio, Kathleen Turner, Dick Cavett, Philip Bosco, Shannen Doherty), by far the most visible and lucrative is Howard Stern who reupped his Sirius contract in December 2010 for five years for five hundred million dollars. His contract is up momentarily. Stern and Buchwald have even more lucrative options this time.

DBA executive VP Ricki Olshan oversees the New York office of this vast agency.

Agents: Joanne Nici, David Lewis, Jonathan Mason, Ricki Olshan, Kevin McEleney and Kaitlyn Flynn
Client List: 1, 016 all departments

Fifi Oscard Agency, Inc.

110 W 40th Street #2100
New York, NY 10018
1-212-764-1100
fifioscard.com

The legendary Fifi Oscard died in 2006. A frustrated housewife and mother in 1949 when she began working gratis for Lee Harris Draper, she said she was inept when she started her job, but quickly became proficient and worked herself up to $15 a week within nine months.

The agency is now in the hands of managing partner lit agent Peter Sawyer and theatrical agent vice-president Carmen LaVia.

When Carmen came to New York from Las Vegas (with wife Arlene Fontana) looking for a job in the business, he began at an amazing level, lucking into a job as an assistant to legendary producer Leland Hayward. When Leland became ill, the office cut back and Carmen joined Fifi. Three years later he joined the William Morris Agency, where he stayed for ten years before coming back home to Fifi.

Carmen and Francis Del Duca rep Philip Hernandez (*Gotham*), Tony Musante (*We Own the Night*) and Kim Brockington (*School of Rock*) and the rest of their theatrical list.

FOA also reps directors, producers, singers, composers and actors. In short, they deal with every aspect of showbiz except the variety field.

Agents: Carmen La Via and Francis Del Duca
Client List: 14 listed at IMBdPro

Frontier Booking International, Inc.

1560 Broadway. #512
New York, NY 10036
1-212-221-0220
frontierbooking.com

When the late Ian Copeland created FBI in 1979, FBI was known as one of the largest rock agencies around ultimately repping Sting, Snoop Doggy Dog, Modern English, and Jane's Addiction, not to mention their very first acting client, Courtney Cox.

When the theatrical department was born in 1984, that department become the dominant presence. FBI reps everyone from Broadway (*Billy Elliot, Mary Poppins, etc.*) to the next generation of television stars.

John Shea (SEM&M and Kronick, Kelly & Lauren) heads up the theatrical department representing a hot list of young actors. Clients from that list include Jacqueline Torres (*FX, Hack*), Sean Nelson (*Deadbeat, Fresh, American Buffalo, The Corner*), Steven Lee Merkel (*Nurse Jackie*), Conor Romero (*Michael J. Fox Show*), Alicia Sable (*Alpha House*), Bitaly Benko (*The Americans*), Daniella DeJesus (*Orange is the New Black*) and Tommy Walker (*Daredevil*).

Heather Finn (Abrams Artists) helps John run herd on their talented bunch. FBI handles all types for all areas. They work with an extensive freelance list in addition to their signed clients.

Agents: John Shea and Heather Finn
Client List: 60 plus freelance

The Gersh Agency New York

41 Madison Ave., 3rd fl.

New York, NY 10010

1-212-997-1818

gershagency.com

The Gersh Agency was started by Phil Gersh in 1949, and in June 2015, *The Hollywood Reporter* listed Gersh in their guide to the seven major Agencies. Led today by Phil's sons, co-presidents Bob and David Gersh and senior managing partner Leslie Siebert, Gersh has managed to retain its family identity, foist off threats from corporations and still be named to that lofty list.

The Gersh Agency represents actors, directors, writers, producers, below-the-line personnel, authors, commercial and voiceover talent. Gersh also has a solid comedy division sporting four agents. The list of agents is vast, so check IMDbPro for more intel.

The bi-coastal client list shared by The Gersh Agency is outstanding featuring 2015 Oscar winners Patricia Arquette and J. K. Simmons as well as Kristen Stewart, Kyle Chandler, John Goodman, Catherine Keener, Adam Driver, Allison Janney, Taylor Schilling, D. L. Hugley, Dave Chappelle, Sam Rockwell, Luis Guzman and others.

Marianne Ways heads the Comedy Department. For the majors list, check hollywoodreporter.com/news/thr-guide-7-major-hollywood-799743).

Agents: Scott Yoselow, Stephen Hirsh, Rhonda Price, Randi Goldstein, Jason Gutman, Seth Glewen, Samantha Chalk, Joyce Ketay, Tara Kromer, Lindsay Porter, Scott Swiontek, Marianne Ways. Elizabeth Wilderselm, Laura Wilkerson, Kyetay Beckner and Rachel Zeldman
Client List: 2160

Ginger Dicce Talent

PO Box 6674
New York, NY 10150
1-212-869-9650
no website

Ginger Dicce has a long memory. When I walked into her office she reminded me that early in our careers, she had cast me in a *Tender Vittles* commercial when she was a commercial producer.

Though I had a tough time getting her on the phone, Ms. Dicce couldn't have been nicer when we met. Even though she was very busy that day, she still made time to tell me about her business.

One of the few agents in town who still works exclusively freelance, Dicce says she still gives newcomers a chance and looks at every piece of mail that enters her office.

Starting as a secretary in advertising, Ginger moved into production via her smarts and helpful mentors. Once she was producing and casting, she says she fell in love with actors and decided to become an agent.

She started her agency in 1986 and has been busily repping union and non-union actors ever since. When I asked Ginger what attracted her to an actor she said it was an "inner gut thing," so your guess is as good as mine. Since Ginger suffers no fools, I wouldn't call her unless you are focused, business oriented, and have some idea how you can be marketed.

Agent: Ginger Dicce
Client List: Freelance

Gotham Talent Agency

200 W 41st St. #1001
New York, NY 10036
1-212-944-8898
gothamtalentagency.com

I first met Cynthia Katz as a client back in the day when she was starting her career repping kids at Abrams Artists. By the time I was profiling agents, she was heading up the east coast offices of Robert Malcolm's agency, The Artists Group East.

She ran that office for 15 years until November of 2009 when she was conscripted to start Gotham Talent Agency. GTA's terrific client list includes Tom Hewitt (*Doctor Zhivago*), Michelle Federer (*Wicked*), Phil Burke (*Hell on Wheels*), Mike Pniewski (*The Good Wife, Secretary, Blue Bloods*), Sol Miranda (*Unbreakable: Kimmy Schmidt*), Peggy Scott (*Show Me a Hero*) and Adam McNulty (*The Path*).

Gotham has a nice website with actual information and Cynthia has no preference on submissions.

Agent: Cynthia Katz
Client List: 40

Hanns Wolters International

599 11th Avenue, 3rd Floor
New York, NY 10036
1-212-714-0100
hannswolters.com

German talent agent Hanns Wolters was initially a British orchestra impresario and also booked Marlene Dietrich's early career as a hand and leg model. The fascinating story of his life, including his escape from Hitler, is on the history tab of the website.

Hanns opened this agency in 1962 and was initially known for his stable of talented European actors, but over time his list expanded. When his wife, actress Marianne Wolters (Mitzi Bera-Monna), died in the 1990s, one of his German actors, Oliver Mahrdt, became Hanns' unofficial son, helping him not only recover from Marianne's death but refocus his business.

Oliver ultimately supported Hanns through his own lengthy fatal illness and now owns the agency. He has put together a treasure trove of information on their website featuring Oliver-produced actor tutorials that are worth checking out.

Still one of the places casting directors call for European actors, but also known for its strong New York character types, HWI works with about 300 union and non-union actors.

This agency doesn't sign contracts with its clients, preferring to work on a handshake basis. They also represent German cinema on the East Coast. Amongst HWI's illustrious projects was Foreign Language Film Oscar winner *Nowhere in Africa*.

The indispensable Bill Duey has been with HWI for 15 years and handles most of the day to day business.

Agents: Bill Duey and Oliver Mahrdt
Client List: 68 listed on IMDbPro

Harden-Curtis Associates

214 W 29th Street, #1203

New York, NY 10001

hardencurtis.com

1-212-977-8502

In 1996 after fifteen years in the business, Mary Harden and Nancy Curtis opened HCA combining the talents of each into this respected agency. Nancy's MA in advertising from Michigan State University and a childhood spent studying acting give Nancy an acting/marketing background edge few agents possess. Mary Harden's early experiences problem solving with writers and actors in a variety of regional theatre jobs provided her contacts and nurturing skills that pay off for her literary clients.

Before joining HCA in 1997, Diane Riley was in casting at The Roundabout Theatre Company and in company management at the Goodspeed Opera House. Northwestern theatre grad Michael Kirsten came aboard the same year and became a VP in 2009. Scott Edwards, a graduate of the Theatrical Design Department of Texas State University, joined the company in 2001.

Clients include Hunter Bell, Veanne Cox, K Todd Freeman, Anita Gillette, Megan Lawrence, Christiane Noll, Hunter Bell, Randy Danson, Lisa Emery, Crystal Dickinson, Damon Gupton, Terrell Tilford, Sharon Wilkins, Boris McGiver, Alysia Reiner and David Alan Basche. The HC client list includes Tony, Obie, Audelco and NAACP Image awards nominees.

Agents: Nancy Curtis, Mary Harden, Diane Riley, Michael Kirsten and Scott Edwards

Client List: 150

Hartig Hilepo Agency

54 W 21st Street. #610
New York, NY 10010
1-212-929-1772
hartighilepo.com

Paul Hilepo was a student at NYU when he was first exposed to the agency business as an intern at Don Buchwald & Associates. When he graduated in 1992, he sent out resumes to various talent agencies and met and clicked with Michael Hartig. He was a franchised agent two years later.

Hartig established this agency in the early 60s and ran it for forty years until his death in 2004 and now Paul is the new owner.

Liz Rosier joined HH in 2006 from theatre management with both ART and Trinity Rep. Their colleague is New York native Peter Sanfilippo (Innovative Artists).

HH's impressive list of clients includes Laverne Cox (*Orange Is the New Black*), Jerry Stiller (*King Of Queens*), Ken Leung (*Star Wars: the Force Awakens*), Phyllis Somerville (*Outsiders*), Samrat Chakrabarti (*In Treatment*), Amy Spanger (*Elf*), Lisa Brescia (*Mamma Mia*), Alli Mauzey (*Wicked*), Kacie Sheik (*Hair*), Patti D'arbanville (*Morning Glory*), James Saito (Life of Pi) and Jaime Cepero (*Smash*).

Paul says he looks carefully at every picture and resume that comes in: "We can't afford to leave any stone unturned. We find clients in many ways, we check out plays, television shows shooting here, and referrals from people we respect." He says he has found clients from blind submissions.

Agents: Paul Hilepo, Liz Rosier and Peter Sanfilippo
Client List: 100

Henderson-Hogan Agency

850 7th Avenue, #1003

New York, NY 10019

1-212-765-5190

no website

Both Maggie Henderson and Jerry Hogan are gone now and the new owner is Jerry's longtime protégé, George Lutsch. George started his career as receptionist-assistant at this iconic bicoastal agency founded by Maggie in 1967.

George's BFA in acting from NYU was the springboard for his first showbiz foray interning with the Royal Court Theatre in London. When he decided to change the direction of his career, he joined Jerry and the rest is history.

George's next in command, Alex Butler, grew up in the city playing guitar and attracted to all things showbiz, so it follows that while he pursued his Philosophy degree from SUNY Purchase, his friends were actors and musicians. After graduation Alex worked briefly at a law firm until his friend George mentioned that he had an opening at HH and Alex finally got into showbusiness where he belonged.

Henderson-Hogan's newest agent, Chad Pisetsky (Bauman, Redanty and Shaul) earned a degree in directing from the University of Michigan.

Clients from their list include Dakin Matthews (*Bridge of Spies*), Jade Wu (*Luke Cage*), David Pegram (*WarHorse*), Peter Jay Fernandez (*Cyrano*), David Harris (*His Dying Wish*) and Christopher Innvar *(The Gershwin's Porgy and Bess)*.

Agents: George Lutsch, Alex Butler and Chad Pisetsky
Client List: 77

Hybrid Agency

353 W 48th St., 3rd floor
New York, NY 10036
1-201-819-7785
thehybridagency.com

Rikky Fishbein played baseball from age 4 through college and planned to be a sport's agent but when he realized he really should have a law degree for that field, his dream began to transition toward the entertainment industry. Upon graduation, he applied to several agencies and chose DDO from the many offers. Rikky says that seeing one of his clients in a show is a feeling he can't even describe or ever replace.

Though he planned to be at DDO a year or so, he was there for four. At that point, Innovative offered him a job. Though he loved DDO, he told his boss that he'd always wanted to be at a big agency and wanted to see what it was like. With their blessing, he moved to Innovative and lived the *Entourage* life. Though he enjoyed that life, he began to yearn for a simpler life with more regular hours.

While weighing his next options, his lawyer suggested he start his own agency where he could make his own hours and rules. Though this initially seemed like crazy talk, Rikky slowly began to realize he had the ability and connections to create an intimate agency back in New York that would be a cross between an agency and manager where every client would get hands on attention: Hybrid.

Rikky is selective about his clients and only has about 60. Some from his list include Betsy Struxness (*Hamilton*), Tracy Shayne (*The Affair, Chorus Line, Les Miz, Phantom*) and Megan Sikira (*Curtains, The Bleeder*). Electronic submissions only to info@hybridagency.com.

Agent: Rikky Fishbein
Clients: 60ish

ICM Partners

730 Fifth Avenue
New York, NY 10019
1-212-556-5665
icmpartners.com

ICM Partners is one of the world's largest talent and literary agencies with offices in New York, Los Angeles and London representing talent in motion pictures, television, books, music, live performance, branded entertainment and new media.

ICM was formed in 1975 through the merger of Creative Management Associates and International Famous Agency. In 2012, the agency completed a management buyout and formed a partnership with the new name ICM Partners.

Led by an entourage of powerful partners, ICM Partners continually jockeys with CAA and WME for the title as the #1 corporate agency in the business.

There appears to be no hierarchy among the partners but just as our credits identify us, agent client lists do the same for agents. If you check each list, you can draw your own conclusions. Toni Howard, Michael Kagan, Lorrie Bartlett, John Burnham, Eddie Yablans, Hildy Gottlieb, Chuck James are just few of names from the illustrious partner list.

Clients include James Spader, Michael Keaton, Robert Duval, Kathy Bates, Chris Rock, Shondra Rhimes, Jay Leno, Michael Caine, Edie Falco, Nathan Lane and John Cusack.

No matter which agent is responsible for you, it's clear that ICM Partners is an astute choice for anyone with the credits and/or heat to compete with their stable of luminous clients.

Agents: Adam Schweitzer, Lawrence Stuart, Bart Walker, Christina Bazdekis, Bonnie Bernstein, Ayala Cohen and others
Client List: 2186

Ingber & Associates

140 Broadway, # 907
New York, NY 10001
1-212-889-9450
no website

Carole Ingber worked in motion picture advertising before moving to Los Angeles to work in casting with Vicki Rosenberg in 1982. When she returned from the West Coast, she worked at a succession of high profile commercial agencies: J. Michael Bloom, SEM&M, LW2 and headed the commercial division of Susan Smith's distinguished agency before opening her own office in 1993.

Although I&A is a commercial agency, I include them because they specialize in handling commercial careers of working actors and also handle industrials.

Carole may be the woman to talk to if you are already working good jobs as an actor and are looking for someone to handle the commercial part of your business.

Agent: Carole Ingber
Client List: 55

Innovative Artists

235 Park Avenue South
New York, NY 10003
1-212-253-6900
innovativeartists.com

It was 1982 when Gersh alums Scott Harris and the late Howard Goldberg opened the West Coast office of Robert Abrams (Abrams Harris & Goldberg). When Abrams exited, it became Harris & Goldberg. Then, after Howard passed away, the present name was chosen. In 1992, Innovative opened the NY office adding literary and production departments and has continued to grow over the years, branching into voiceover, commercials, beauty, comedy, hosting and speakers.

Along with agency owner and president Scott Harris, Innovative Artists is managed by an executive committee comprised of executive vice president Nevin Dolcefino; vice presidents: Maury DiMauro, Gary Gersh, Debbie Haeusler, Jonathan Howard, Marcia Hurwitz; and general counsel Jon Coronel. IA has a staff of 68.

Clients include Pamela Reed, Bill Irwin, Kate Mulgrew, Wendie Malick, Mary McDonnell, Sissy Spacek, Amanda Seyfried, Paul Guilfoyle, Rita Moreno, Ann Cusack, Bob Newhart and Lorraine Bracco.

Agents: Gary Gersh, Courtney Borrensen, Benjamin Carnegie, Brian Davidson, Allan Duncan, Allie Flauter, Ross Haime, Marla Haut, Shari Hoffman, Bill Veloric and more
Client List: 2342

Jim Flynn, Inc.

225 W 23rd St., 5P

New York, NY 10011

1-212-868-1068

no website

Jim Flynn entered show business in 1990 answering phones at Susan Smith's agency. His first agenting job was at the New York Agency which merged with Alliance Talent. In 1995 he and Judy Boals came together to create Berman, Boals & Flynn, one of the most effective talent and literary agencies in town. At that time they were partnered with literary icon Lois Berman.

In the spring of 2003, after seven years as partners, Judy and Jim mutually decided they wanted their own agencies; they are still great friends.

Somehow Jim has managed to maintain a successful talent/literary agency and attend law school at the same time. In 2003 he earned the right to sign "Esq." after his name. As a lawyer he can add entertainment law to his list of services, a big plus for clients. Flynn's list of actors includes Vincent Rodriquez III (*Crazy Ex-Girlfriend*).

Though this is a wonderful agency to aspire to, Jim says he isn't looking for any clients right now, so save your postage.

Agent: Jim Flynn
Client List: 30

Jordan Gill & Dornbaum Agency

1370 Broadway, 5th Fl.
New York, NY 10018
1-212-463-8455
jgdtalent.com

Although Robin Dornbaum loved actors and wanted to work with them some way, she never knew how until she interned with the legendary Marje Fields while still in school as a communications major. At that point Robin knew she had found her calling. After six months, mentor Fields sent her to work in casting at Reed Sweeney Reed, where she worked for free, honed her skills, stored information and grew in the business. After graduation, she got a job at The Joe Jordan Agency.

Within three years Robin was President and brought in Jeffrey Gill (Bonni Kidd, Fifi Oscard) as her partner. Their combination of youth, savvy and industriousness changed this agency into one of the top child and young adult agencies in New York.

Former actor David McDermott (FBI, HWA) reps the eighteen to thirty age group and is interested in special skills (skateboarders, all types of athletes, dancers, little people, beatboxers, etc.). Jeff heads the legit department, while Robin reps the commercial clients.

Clients include Ruby Jerins (*Nurse Jackie, Remember Me, Shutter Island*), Sterling Jerins (*Divorce, World War Z, The Conjuring, No Escape, Geostorm*), Ian Nelson (*Teen Wolf, Legends, The Hunger Games, The Boy next Store, Like Me, Freak Show*), Julia Goldani Telles (*Bunheads, The Affair, Whitney*), Jonny Weston (*Chasing Mavericks, Kelly & Cal, Project Almanac, Taken 3, Insurgent, We are your Friends, Beyond Skyline*), Maxwell Simkins (*And So it Goes, Love the Coopers, The book of Henry*) and Charlie Kilgore (*Divorce*).

Agents: Robin Dornbaum, Jeffrey Gill and David McDermott
Client List: 61

Judy Boals, Inc.

307 W 38th Street, #812
New York, NY 10018
1-212-500-1424
judyboals.com

Judy Boals started in the business as an actor, but a part-time job working in varying capacities with literary legend Lois Berman ultimately led not only to her agenting career, but also to a partnership with Berman and talent/literary agent Jim Flynn (Susan Smith, The New York Agency, Alliance Talent) in 1995.

Berman died in January of 2003 and that spring, after seven years as partners, Boals and Flynn mutually decided they wanted their own agencies. But since they were friends, they decided to share space.

Names from Judy's list include David Mogentale, David Greenspan, Daren Kelly, Winston Duke, Taylor Mac, Marc Webster, Laurence Mason, Alet Taylor and Dena Tyler.

Boals continues to represent actors, composers/songwriters, directors and writers who are chosen not only for their talent, but because they are easy to get along with.

Agent: Judy Boals
Client List: 50

Kazarian, Measures, Ruskin & Associates

110 W 40th St., #2506
New York, NY 10018
1-212-582-7572
kmrtalent.com

Growing up on Long Island, Jed Abrahams went to a performing arts high school and on to the NYU Tisch musical theatre program, then worked professionally on national tours. He says he spent his 20s working as a singing waiter at a steak house where he formulated many skills he still uses today as an agent.

From the steakhouse to a 2 week internship at Henderson-Hogan that resulted in a job, Jed has never looked back. From his stint at HH, he moved to Stewart Talent and then Talent House before being tapped to head up the NY offices of KMR. Jed says he values his journey that has finally led him to his "place."

Moving from boutique agencies to a larger bicoastal agency has not changed Jed's style. His focus is to keep his theatrical list small and retain the family/boutique vibe he brought with him with an emphasis on focusing on nurturing established performers.

Colleagues Ashley Landay was at Professional Artists for 9 years while Cassandra Tay started her agenting career at KMR as an intern and is newly franchised. Ashley is from Colorado and Cassandra from New Jersey. Clients include Chip Zien (*Into the Woods*), Alison Fraser (*The Secret Garden, Happish*), Lisa Howard (*It Should Have Been You*), Liz Larsen (*The Most Happy Fellow*), Ali Stroker (*Glee*), John Wesley Shipp (The Flash), Sean Cullen (*House of Cards),* Jake Silbermann (*The Essembled Parties*), Sasha Allen (*The Voice*) and Joanna P. Adler (*Devious Maids*).

Currently focused on nurturing established performers, KMR isn't looking for developmental clients. They prefer snail mail in any case.

Agents: Jed Abrahams, Ashley Landay and Cassandra Tay
Client List: 80

The Krasny Office, Inc.

1501 Broadway, #1507
New York, NY 10019
1-212-730-8160
no website

Gary Krasny has a valuable background for an agent. He was an actor, a publicist for Berkeley Books, a story editor for Craig Anderson (after he left the Hudson Theatre Guild) and an assistant to Broadway general manager Norman Rothstein at Theatre Now. In 1985 he decided he was more empathetic with the artist than management and decided to become an agent.

Gary honed his agenting skills at various agencies before opening his own in late 1991. He found office space not only in the same building, but on the same floor where he had worked with Craig Anderson years before.

Gary's background, experience and taste made him a favorite with the casting community and he became part of the mainstream as soon as he opened his office.

He runs the legit department along with colleague B. Lynne Jebens (Michael Hartig) and Mikey Nagy. Mikey, who hails from Ohio, came to New York as an actor. After meeting Gary at a seminar, he began interning at Krasny and moved up to junior associate and now franchised agent.

Clients from their list include Denny Dillon (*Dream On*), Cathy Trien, Laura Kenyon, Marcus Paul James, Jim Brochu and Ken Jennings. The Krasny Office has liaison arrangements with several Los Angeles agents and managers.

Agents: Gary Krasny, B. Lynne Jebens and Mikey Nagy
Client List: 61

Lally Talent Agency/LTA

630 9th Avenue, #800
New York, NY 10038
1-212-974-8718
no website

Dale Lally was an actor and personal manager before he crossed the desk to become an agent. He worked for Mary Ellen White and Nobel Talent before partnering with print agents Wallace Rogers and Peter Lerman (Lally Rogers & Lerman). When Lally, Rogers and Lerman decided to go their separate ways in 1992, Dale opened this office.

Partner Stephen Laviska worked in contract law before he joined Dale in representing their strong list of musical performers, interesting young adults, and solid character people.

Actors from their list include Jerome Preston Bates, Kalpo Schwab, Alice Spivak, Elysia Segal, Gary Evans and Gerry Sheridan.

I never got an answer from Dale when I called, so this is based on my last conversation with him and IMDbPro.

Agents: Dale Lally and Stephen Laviska
Client List: 45

Leading Artists, Inc.

145 W 45th Street, #1000
New York, NY 10036
1-212-391-4545
no website

Owner Dianne Busch came to New York from Ohio in 1979 figuring to act, but soon found a cross-section of showbiz jobs she liked, ranging from casting commercials with Joy Weber to legit with Meg Simon. A brief stint as a manager led the way to agenthood at Silver, Massetti and Szatmary in 1991. When Monty Silver retired 12 years later, Dianne bought the agency and changed the name to Leading Artists, Inc.

Colleagues Diana Doussant (Talentworks) and Michael Kelly Boone help guide the careers of Zeljko Ivanek (*Madame Secretary*), Gregory Jbara (*Blue Bloods*), Paul Fitzgerald (*VEEP*), Richard Masur (*Transparent*), Ron Cephas Jones (*Mr. Robot, The Get Down*), Susan Kelechi Watson (*Louie, VEEP*), Matthew Rauch (*Banshee*), Adriane Lenox (*Blacklist, The Blind Side*), Afton Williamson (*The Breaks, Nashville, Banshee*), Jayne Houdyshell (*The Humans, Law & Order: SVU*), Larry Pine (*House of Cards*), Nina Lisandrello (*Beauty & The Beast*), J.C. MacKenzie (*Vinyl, House of Cards*), Brooks Ashmanskas (*Something Rotten, The Good Wife*), Eisa Davis (*House of Cards*), A.J. Shively (*Bright Star*), Rosie Benton (*Curious Incident…*), Teresa Avia Lim (*Awake and Sing!*), David Gregory (*Deception*), Chuck Cooper (*House of Cards, Amazing Grace*), Nick Dillenburg (*Orange Is The New Black*), Marceline Hugot (*The Leftovers*), Finnerty Steeves (*DOT*), Edward Baker-Duly (*The King & I*), Leon Addison Brown (*The Knick, Misery*), Ivan Martin (*Billions*), Ben Jeffrey (*The Lion King*), Rashidra Scott (*Beautiful*), Brian Sears (*Book of Mormon*), Daniel Oreskes (*HIR*), Lisa Banes (*Girl Gone*). Leading Artists is affiliated with LA agencies SMS Talent and SDB Partners.

Agents: Dianne Busch, Michael Kelly Boone and Diana Doussant
Client List: 118

Lionel Larner, Ltd.

130 E 75th Street, #12D

New York, NY 10021

1-212-628-3242

no website

Lionel Larner grew up in London and Wiltshire attending the Italia Conti Academy of Theatre Arts, Britain's oldest theatre arts training school. He was the office boy in a theatre started by Sir Richard Attenborough before joining the casting department of ITV and the BBC.

His job as European casting director for the Otto Preminger film *St. Joan* was instrumental in his move to New York where he started a new life as an agent. He was trained by CAA's legendary Martin Baum while they were both at GAC. In 1969, when Lionel left Baum and GAC (now ICM), he started Lionel Larner, Ltd.

The Tiffany of agents, Lionel has always had a glittering client list led by Diana Riggs and Glenda Jackson, to name a couple. Ms. Jackson left acting to be a Member of Parliament for twenty years, but has now retired to return to acting and to Lionel who never took her name from his list.

When longtime friend and client Dorothy Loudon died, she named Lionel to run her foundation which is why Lionel keeps his list small and isn't really looking to add to it. Electronic submissions only lionellarner@gmail.com and no dropins, please.

Agents: Lionel Larner
Client List: 3

Luedtke Agency

1674 Broadway, #7A
New York, NY 10019
1-212-765-9564
no website

Penny Luedtke has been in some kind of showbiz related job since she was twelve, but her entrance into the agency business came because she is such a stalwart friend. When an acquaintance who owned a classical music management company asked her to run his office for a few weeks while he was in Europe on business, Penny demurred at first, but finally acquiesced and was surprised by how much she enjoyed the work.

To learn the agency business, she approached children's agent Pat Gilchrist in 1996 about starting an adult department at her agency. When Penny opened her own office a year later, her multi-talented friends all wanted to be clients so she determined to represent not only actors, but writers and directors as well. Her acting client list includes Emma Myles, Doug E. Doug, James Robinson, Shirley Knight and Todd Susman.

New Yorker Mike Cruz was at Independent Artists and Cyd LeVin & Associates management before becoming Penny's colleague. Penny and Mike prefer electronic submissions: luedeke@luedekeagency.

Agents: Penny Luedtke and Mike Cruz
Client List: 125

Nicolosi & Co. Inc.

150 W 25ᵗʰ Street, #1200
New York, NY 10001
1-212-633-1010
nicolosi-co.com

After getting a B.A. in acting from UMass and an MA in both acting and directing from Emerson College, Jeanne Nicolosi taught acting and headed the theatre department at a Boston high school. She moved to New York in the late 70s to act and direct and though she found success at both, she wanted more control over her career and to coach and develop others. Her first exposure as an assistant agent with Beverly Anderson convinced her she was on that path.

In 1985 Jeanne became a franchised agent, working briefly at Writers & Artists before joining The Bob Waters Agency where she became a partner while continuing to hone her talent and business management skills. Ultimately envisioning her own agency, Nicolosi's dream was realized in 2002 when she opened Nicolosi & Company, Inc. She met all her first year goals and continues to grow. Nicolosi's modern website featuring news of her clients and reviews from casting directors reflects her understanding of the importance of online communication.

Ex-thesp David Cash (Henderson-Hogan, CESD, Harter Manning Woo) and Jeremy Leiner join Jeanne in repping her impressive list of actors for Broadway, film and television. Mariann Mayberry (*Steppenwolf*), Marina Squerciati (*Chicago PD*), Chelsea Spack (*Gotham*), Li Jun Li (*Minority Report, Quantico*), Kim Director (*Blair Witch Project 2*), Julia Murney (*Wicked*), Ben Fankhauser (*Beautiful*), Dan DeLuca (*Newsies*), Emily Cramer (*School of Rock*), Joaquina Kalukango (*The Color Purple*) and Brandon Uranowitz (*An American in Paris*).

Agents: Jeanne Nicolosi , David Cash and Jeremy Leiner
Client List: 76

Meg Pantera, The Agency

138 W 15th Street, First Floor
New York City, NY 10011
1-212-219-9330
megpanteratheagency.com

Meg Pantera was the artistic director at Buffalo's The Theatre Of Youth Company and also at the Rochester Association of Performing Arts before she followed a new love to the Big Apple in 1990. A friend suggested she would make a good agent so she signed on for a part time stint with Bob Barry (Barry Haft Brown) and was franchised five years later. She opened her own agency in January 2000.

Meg feels the partnership between an actor and an agent is forged by mutual hard work and respect. In a time when boutique agencies are failing, hers thrives. She says she prizes the close relationships she has developed with her clients helping them develop their careers.

Clients include Drew Sarich (*Rocky the New Musical*), Paul Whitty (*Once*), Brian J. Keane (*War Horse, Lights Out*), Kenita Miller (*Once on this Island, Color Purple*), Geno Segers (*Pair of Kings*), Nathan Lee Graham (*Priscilla Queen of the Desert, Wild Party*), Patricia Buckley (*Evolution*), Abigail Savage (*Precious*), Ramsey Farallagallah (*Homeland*), Zainab Jah (*The Convert*) and actor-director-respected teacher of Michael Chekhov technique, Lenard Petit.

Colleague Katie Murphy graduated from Nazareth College of Rochester with a BS in Musical Theatre. She started working with Meg in 2012 and is now a subagent.

Meg and Katie attend showcases, readings and accept submissions. Check their website for more details.

Agents: Meg Pantera and Katie Murphy
Client List: 75

Metropolis Artists Agency

2008 E 30ᵗʰ St.

New York City, NY 10016

1-212-779-0814

metropolisagency.com

Polish musician Marius Bargielski's first showbiz jobs in film and television production schooled him in the business and provided lots of travel, but his music career was really his focus so he left production work and began to concentrate on his music.

Though in 1991 he came to the US for that reason, he found himself connecting his actor and musician friends with jobs via his New York contacts and realized he had a talent and an interest in artist management, as well.

In 2008, he decided to focus on that part of himself and opened his agency. He reps clients for film, television and theatre as well as for commercials, print and voice overs.

Clients from his list include Jay Beecher (*Taken 3, As the World Turns, Third Watch, Law & Order, Patient Zero, The Shield, Once and Again*), Brigitte Millar (*Harry Potter and the Order of the Phoenix, Spectre*), Philippe Reinhardt (*Stalingrad, Max*) and Amr El-Bayoumi (*Captain Phillips, Madame Secretary, Blacklist, Person of Interest, Mr. Robot, House of Cards*).

MAA accepts submissions via both emails and snail mail.

Agent: Marius Bargielski

Clients: 129

Paradigm

360 Park Avenue South, 16th Floor
New York, NY 10110
1-212-897-6400
paradigmagency.com

In 1982, LA Agent Sam Gores started SGA (Sam Gores Agency) with 25 clients. In the ensuing 30 plus years, Sam merged or acquired Jack Fields, STE, ATM & Associates, literary agencies Robinson, Weintraub & Gross and Shorr, Stille & Associates and music agencies Monterey Peninsula Artists, Little Big Man, AM Only and Coda Music and is now known as Paradigm.

This major conglomerate now has offices in LA, NY, Monterey and Nashville with departments of motion picture, television, music, comedy, personal appearances, theatre, books, new media, commercial and physical production. Sam has increased his client list size more than 100 times.

Actors on his list include Shailene Woodley, Alison Janney, Julie Bowen, Richard Schiff, Mark Harmon, Antonio Banderas, Andy Garcia, Laurence Fishburne, Jonathan Frakes, Courtney Thorne-Smith, Willie Garson and Susan Sullivan.

In spite of Paradigm's colossal size and power, Gores was quoted in *Billboard* in 2014 saying, "I like to think we're in the client business, not necessarily the agent business. I don't think we've ever made a move that could be good for the agency but not good for the artist. We've never leveraged a client in that way."

Sarah Fargo is head of the theatrical division in New York. Agents who represent actors in New York are listed below.

Agents: Sarah Fargo, Matthew Kaplan, Kevin Kastrup, Tim Sage, Richard Schmenner, Scott Metzger, Jamie Hughes, Ellen Gilbert, John Domingos, Rachel Altman, Kevin Kastrup, Ed Micone and others
Client List: 2165

People Store

645 Lambert Drive
Atlanta GA 30324
1-404-874-6448

peoplestore.net

These days with business spread all over the country, sometimes actors have agents spread all over the country too so I'm covering Atlanta based People Store which has been getting work for a lot of New York actors. Though I contacted PS, they never got back to me so this is written entirely via research.

People Store emerged from the brain of former stylist and production coordinator Rebecca Shrager. As Atlanta boomed as a production center, she decided to organize and support the local talent. She took her contacts and background from the Atlanta College of Art into the streets and local theatre companies photographing interesting faces and building this untapped talent pool into the fabric of Atlanta's entertainment business.

People Store merged with The Talent Group and Hot Shot Kids in 2002 and with Quantum Events and Entertainment in 2010 and in 2012 they opened a branch in New Orleans, so they cover a lot of territory and a variety of jobs.

Brenda Pauley heads the film department and is joined by her colleagues listed below in repping their busy client list that includes Jena Sims (*Kill the Messenger*), Catherine Taber (*Star Wars: The Clone Wars*), Dominique Perry (*Get Hard*) and Eddie Steeples (*My Name is Earl*).

I could never get a return phone call or e-mail from People Store so this is written totally from research.

Agents: Rebecca Shrager, Brenda Pauley, Jessie Alfonso, Victoria Temple, Brenda Pauley, Milam Thompson and Kristina Sutton
Clients: 385

Phoenix Artists

330 W 38th St, # 607
New York, NY 10018
1-212-586-9110
no website

When Gary Epstein was a kid and the *Sound of Music* was playing on Broadway, his pro-active-singer mom managed an audition for Gary so that he might follow in her footsteps. Gary said the stage manager actually said, "Don't call us, we'll call you."

They never did, but Gary immediately started studying acting and performing in local and children's theatre companies. After graduation from Hofstra University, though he landed some acting jobs, a chance day job with the Mort Schwartz Agency opened his eyes to another way to be in show business. He worked with Mort for a year before joining the legendary NY agent Stark Hesseltine (Hesseltine-Baker) in 1978. When Baker died in 1986, Gary opened Phoenix Artists.

In 1991 seeking a bicoastal presence, Gary began a long partnership with Los Angeles agent Craig Wyckoff (Epstein/Wyckoff and later Epstein Wyckoff Corsa Ross & Associates). When that partnership dissolved in 2005, Phoenix Artists rose again.

Veteran Randi Ross continues with Gary. Their colleague Dolores Williams is an attorney who yearned to work in show business. She interned at another agency before coming to Phoenix where she climbed the ladder from intern to assistant to agent.

Phoenix is primarily a theatrical agency servicing actors in all parts of the business. Their small literary list of writers and directors are either old friends or actor clients who became hyphenates and asked Gary to shepherd their careers so no need to query in that area. Gary won't let me name names so check IMDbPro.

Agents: Gary Epstein, Randi Ross and Dolores Williams
Client List: 84

The Price Group Talent

33 W 9th St, 4th floor
New York, NY 10011
1-212 725-1980
thepricegrouptalentagency.com

After graduating SUNY Purchase with a Dramatic Arts Degree and an interest in production, Lisa Price moved to San Diego to intern at San Diego Rep. There she cast, directed and assisted both Josephina Lopez on the first production of *Real Women Have Curves* and the theatre's founder and Artistic Director, Sam Woodhouse. She has since cast, acted, directed and produced for a variety of television and theatre projects in both Los Angeles and New York.

A friend's suggestion led Lisa to an ad on www.playbill.com for an assistant's job with iconic talent agent Beverly Anderson. Anderson recognized Lisa's inherent skills, taught her the agency business and encouraged her to be an agent almost immediately. Price left Anderson in 2006 to open her own agency. Today, she also is an industry professional consultant, master class instructor and coach for musical theatre and drama students at several universities and private New York City educational and networking studios for professional actors.

Her clients work Broadway, film, television, national tours, commercials, the web and Vegas. Names from her list include Benny Elledge (*Nerds, Bull Durham, Blue Bloods*), Karina Ortiz (*Orange Is the New Black*), Allen Lewis Rickman (*Public Morals, Boardwalk Empire, A Serious Man*), Coleen Sexton (*Jekyll & Hyde, Wicked, Legally Blonde, Mamma Mia*), Greg Cook (*Person of Interest, Blue Bloods, Elementary*) and Gloria Loring (*Correcting Christmas*).

Price only reps talent age 18 and over. Her website celebrates her clients and has great tips for actors during downtime.

Agent: Lisa Price
Client List: 30

Professional Artists

321 W 44th Street, #605
New York, NY 10036
1-212-247-8770
no website

Sheldon Lubliner is fun, easy to talk to, informed, a good negotiator and he has a good client list. Add charm, taste, ability, access and his great partner Marilynn Scott Murphy and you've pretty much got a picture of the Professional Artists vibe.

As a director-producer, Sheldon enjoyed all the details involved in mounting shows for Al Pacino, Gene Barry, and Vivica Lindfors; he just didn't like raising the money.

Deciding he could transfer all his skills into agenting and not be a fundraiser, Sheldon changed careers in 1980, translating his contacts and style into an agency called News and Entertainment. PA is an outgrowth of that venture.

Actress/client Marilynn Scott Murphy was commandeered to answer phones in a pinch in 1984 and in 1987 became a co-owner of PA. Having been a successful actress herself, Marilynn brought with her people skills and knowledge necessary to successfully represent actors in this highly competitive industry.

Colleague Ruthie Christianson, an actress from the midwest whose stint as an intern led her to find that there was another exciting way to be in the business, worked her way up the PA ladder and now helps Sheldon and Marilynn rep their list of respected working actors. A few from their list are Tony Lo Bianco, Kerry O'Malley and Catherine Curtain.

Agents: Sheldon Lubliner, Marilynn Scott and Ruthie Christianson
Client List: 100

The Roster Agency
247 W 38th St, 10th Fl
New York, NY 10018
1-212-725-8459
therosteragency.com.

Michael Rodriguez's BFA in theatre from Southwest Texas State University in 1990 positioned him for his first showbiz job as product manager at Atlantic Records. He worked on albums for Mick Jagger, Bette Midler, Hootie and The Blowfish, Stone Temple Pilots, Tori Amos and Phil Collins among others before founding his own record promotions company in 1996. He learned the agenting business at Hartig Hilipo and DGRW and built and ran Ugly Talent NY prior to starting The Roster Agency in 2005.

Colleague Ellery Sandhu studied acting and musical theatre at Marymount Manhattan College before performing and working as an associate director. Ellery and Michael's paths crossed when she was working as an agent assistant. Ten years later, when he got his own agency, he invited Ellery to be his associate.

Clients from their list include Lori Tan Chinn and Nancy Ticotin (*Gotta Dance*), Bryan Welnicki (*The Bridges of Madison County*), Didi Conn (*Grease*), John Amos (*Madea's Witness Protectin*), Tina Louise (*The Stepford Wives*), Susan Anton (*Baywatch*), Diane Salinger (*Carnivale*) and John Rubinstein (*Pippin, Atlas Shrugged II*).

Agent: Michael Rodriguez
Client List: 50

Sheplin - Winik Artists

888C 8th Ave., #247
New York City, NY 10019
1-646-246-8853
sw-artists.com

Sue Winik comes from a three generation showbiz family. Her mom was Edger Bergen's protégée. Sue was an actor and so was her son from age seven until college. Sue has been an actor, manager and an agent. Originally partnered with H. Shep Pamplin when they created the agency in 2005, when Shep moved to Oklahoma to teach and run a theatre, Sue ultimately enlisted colleagues Margaret Emory and Valerie Adami and moved forward.

Margaret Emory (Dulcina Eisen, Coleman-Rosenberg) graduated from Princeton and the Neighborhood Playhouse. She's a lyricist, a tennis enthusiast and a member of Women in Film. She also created and writes a column for *Backstage*. NY native Valerie Adami's background includes musical theatre, opera, industrial narration and casting for commercials. She was the Director of Weist-Barron film and TV school for 25 years. Valerie heads up the developing Youth Department.

SW Artists rep both union and non-union actors, comedians and young adults for tours, sketch comedy, regional theatre, television and Broadway. Though she says her signed clients come first, she does work with free lance talent. Clients include Jorge Pupo (*Boardwalk Empire*), Lana Neuman (*Sweet Smell of Success*), Christine Dwyer (*Wicked*), "Ellie" Meyer (*Boardwalk Empire*) and Kent Jackman (*Law & Order: SVU*).

Sue has a soft spot for improv actors and comedians and an amazing blog on her website. Be sure to take a look. I was unable to contact her for this edition, so this is as current as can be without talking to her.

Agent: Sue Winik, Margaret Emory and Valerie Adami
Client List: 12 + Freelance

Stone Manners Salners

900 Broadway, #910
New York, NY 10003
1-212-505-1400
smsagency.com

The offspring of a famous British agent, Tim Stone came to Los Angeles in 1979 to provide services for British actors in this country by establishing his own agency, UK Management. Using his British list as a base, Tim's list quickly expanded to represent a much broader range of talent.

In April 1986, Scott Manners (Fred Amsel, Richard Dickens Agency) became Tim's partner. Glenn Salners came aboard as an agent in 2002. Tim moved to New York in 2003 to open the Manhattan office. Glenn became a partner in 2010 and the current bicoastal Stone Manners Salners was born.

Ben Sands started his career as a child actor. He went to college at Boston University and upon graduation became interested in the other aspects of the business. After a series of internships he decided agenting was the perfect fit for him. That led him to a job as an assistant, then he changed agencies and was franchised as an agent in January 2007. He joined Stone Manners Salners in 2011.

Growing up in Southern California and coming to the east coast to attend New York University, Remy Saint Denis always knew the entertainment industry was where his passions lay. He accepted a position as Ben Sands' assistant while he was still in school. Working his way up from there, Remy became an agent in 2014.

SMS won't let me name anyone from their list of actors, directors, producers, scriptwriters, young adults and teens, so you'll have to check for that information.

Agents: Tim Stone, Ben Sands and Remy Saint Denis
Client List: check IMDbPro

Stewart Talent

318 W 53rd St, # 201
Ne York, NY 10019
1-212 315 5505
stewarttalent.com

Chicago agent Jane Stewart created her signature agency in 1980 with a staff of two. Today her empire includes agencies in New York, Atlanta, Chicago and Los Angeles repping actors, theatrical directors and stylists.

Her New York partner Donald Birge was originally an actor who much preferred scoring the job, not working it. It finally occurred to him that agenting would multiply his pleasure at job getting without the drawback of actually having to act. He interned at a couple of NY agencies before joining with Stewart to open their Manhattan office in November of 2004. Since the roots of this distinguished agency are in Chicago, the client list is heavy with Chicago talent that includes *August: Osage County* standouts Rondi Reed and Deanna Dunagan.

Kara Volkmann left her wardrobe career to help Donald open the agency. Colleagues Tim Marshall, Debbi Epstein and Dannielle Quinoa (Innovative Artists, Kazarian Spencer) join him in repping an amazing list that includes Betty Buckley, Carol Kane, Deanna Dunagen, Stephen Wallem, Daniel J. Travanti, Kelly McCreary, James McMenamin, Rose Hemingway and Rusty Schwimmer. You can see their clients and their pictures at their terrific website.

Agents: Donald Birge, Danielle Quinoa, Tim Marshall and Debbi Epstein
Client List: 200

The Talent House

325 W 38th Street # 605
New York, NY 10018
1-212-957-5220
nowebsite

Toronto based, Bruce Dean's Talent House established a New York presence in 1999 and is today helmed by Pete Kaiser (The Gage Group, Henderson-Hogan). Originally an actor, Pete's day job as a bookkeeper at The Gage Group quickly became more interesting than pursuing an acting career so when a full-time job opened up, he switched sides of the desk and quickly became franchised.

Though he relocated to the Los Angeles office in 2002, he couldn't stay away from the Big Apple. He joined Talent House in 2008 and now runs the place with colleague Danny Prather. Like many successful agents, Danny was an actor who interned in a downtime, loved what he found and continued a journey from The Mine to becoming an agent at Peter Strain then on to Buchwald and in 2014 found himself at Talenthouse.

A few from their list are Todd Buonopane (*30 Rock*), Bailey DeYoung (*Faking It*), Donna Lynne Champlin (*Crazy Ex-Girlfriend*), Jennifer Cody (*The Princess and the Frog*), Lusia Strus (*Good Behavior*), Matt McGrath (*Boys Don't Cry*), Henriette Mantel (*Grownups*), Emily Skinner (*Side Show*), Carlos Valdez (*The Flash*) and Tonya Pinkins (*Gotham*).

Agents: Pete Kaiser and Danny Prather
Client List: 90

The Mine

420 Lexington Ave., #628
New York NY 10170
1-212-612-3200
the-mine.com

The agency David Crombie created in 2007 is now helmed by Dustin Flores and Amanda Kouri.

Dustin Flores was head of the musical theatre department at Judy Boals, Inc. before joining the Mine. He reps a client list that includes Marla Mindelle (*Sister Act*), Jeff Kready (*Billy Elliot*), Rachel Potter (*Evita, The Adamms Family*), Trista Moldovan (*Phantom of the Opera*), Rachel Bay Jones (*Women on the Verge of a Nervous Breakdown*), Will Connolly (*Once*), Nic Rouleau (*Book of Mormon*) and Ryan Steele (*Newsies the Musical, Billy Elliot*).

Colleague Amanda Kouri's BA is from Western Carolina University.

Clients mostly come to this agency via referral.

Agents: Dustin Flores and Amanda Kouri
Client List: 90

Talent Representatives, Inc.

1040 First Avenue
New York, NY 10022
1-212-752-1835

Honey Raider and Steve Kaplan's mutual love of theatre, film and television led them to create this agency as a way to become involved in show business. Steve died many years ago, but Honey has managed to survive and prosper on her own. In fact, in 2016 Talent Representatives enters its 52nd year!

Honey maintains a limited list of actors in order to ensure a personal approach. Though the agency was created to represent actors, Honey says many of her actor clients who worked daytime shows decided to write and ended up being staff writers and ultimately producers and directors, so she became their lit agent as well.

Talent Representatives is now one of the few agencies that has a real daytime television literary business. Honey's list of clients is confidential.

Agents: Honey Raider
Client List: 17 plus freelance

Talentworks New York

505 Eighth Avenue #603
New York, NY 10018
1-212-889-0800
talentworksny.com

Jay Kane had stars in his eyes when he arrived in New York to study with Stella Adler at NYU, but after graduation, he assessed his acting range and began searching for another theatre career path. The search took him to New Hampshire's Hampton Playhouse where he grew from teenage apprentice to perennial summer general company and/or stage manager. In the winter he returned to NY, still searching for his place in the business. Working as a business manager at the WPA, as an AD on a Broadway show, and several years in ticket sales at the Metropolitan Opera, Kane turned a deaf ear to friends who kept telling him he'd make a great agent, but in 1990 he embraced his destiny by taking a receptionist job at Select Artists and starting up the ladder. Just three years later he was an agent at The Tantleff Office and in 1998 he joined Talentworks.

Jay's colleagues Danielle Ippolito and Kyle Bosley help him rep the impressive list that includes Michelle Hurd (*The Glades*), Barry Bostwick (*The Rocky Horror Picture Show, Spin City*), Betsy Brandt (*Breaking Bad*), Amy Irving (*Carrie*), Joe Morton (*Scandal*), Karen Ziemba (*Contact*), Carolyn McCormick (*Law & Order*), Michael Berresse (*The Knick*), Ian Kahn (*Turn*), Robert Cuccioli (*Jeckyll & Hyde*) and Amy Irving *(Carrie, Coast of Utopia)*.

Agents: Jay Kane, Danielle Ippolito and Kyle Bosley
Client List: 250 combined coasts

United Talent Agency/UTA

888 Seventh Ave., 9th Fl.

New York, NY 10106

1-212-659-2600

unitedtalent.com

Jeremy Zimmer is the CEO of the powerhouse that leads in every area of entertainment. Originally thought of as the agency for A-list writers and actors, today UTA specializes in A-list everything: writers, comedy, music, broadcast, live entertainment, film, television, independent film, fine arts, literary, production, social media, touring. They have offices in Los Angeles, New York, London, Nashville, Toronto, Miami and Malmö.

Although UTA's webpage is not a fund of information, they do have a tab that names their staggering list of A-list comedy talent. A few of them are Andy Samberg, Bill Hader, Garry Shandling, Sarah Silverman, Seth Meyers, and Wanda Sykes. There are also tabs identifying their music and speakers rosters.

Acting clients include: Benedict Cumberbatch, Scott Eastwood, Johnny Depp, Elizabeth Banks, Kate Mara, Mark Ruffalo, Liev Schreiber, Harrison Ford, Owen Wilson, Joel Coen, Kelsey Grammar, Robert Duvall, Ice Cube, Bryan Cranston, Christopher Guest, Aaron Paul, Corey Stoll.

United Talent is the result of varying mergers and acquisitions over the years discussed in detail earlier in the book.

Agents: Jeremy Zimmer, James Berkus, Rich Klubeck, Tracy Jacobs, Richard Arlook, etc.

Client List: 3143

William Morris Endeavor (WME)

11 Madison Ave.
New York, NY 1001o
1-212-586-5100
wmeentertainment.com

The agency created by Mr. William Morris in 1898 is no more. In the great Endeavor-William Morris merger of 2009, though Endeavor settled for last billing, they pretty much took everything else. Of the three co-CEOs running the place, two are from Endeavor (Ari Emanuel and Patrick Whitesell) and one from WMA (Dave Wirtschafter) so it's easy to see that the 14-year-old upstart Endeavor Agency pretty much told the 111 year old agency how it was going to be.

Until the merger, the William Morris Agency was the longest running entertainment talent agency. Started in 1898 and lasting 118 years, that's still a pretty good run.

WME represents clients in film, television, theatre, music, digital, new media, commercials, literary, comedy, branding & lifestyle, production, lectures, sports, personal appearances, TV-scripted, TV-non-scripted, voice works, video games and pretty much anything else you can name, but if you look at the staff list under titles, more agents are talent agents than anything else.

Stars from their list include Jim Carrey, Mike Myers, Mark Wahlberg, Denzel Washington, Toby Maguire, Oprah Winfrey, Larry David, Michael Moore, Jake Gyllenhaal, Matt Damon, Christian Bale, Ben Affleck, Hugh Jackman, Michelle Williams, Josh Gad, Emma Watson, Keri Russell, Amy Pohler, Jonah Hill, etc.

Agents: Ari Emanuel, Patrick Whitesell, David Lonner, Dan Aloni, Rick Rosen, Adam Venit, Andrew Finkelstein, Nancy Josephson, etc.
Client List: 4,359

Wolf Talent Group

165 W 46th Street, #1104
New York, NY 10036
1-212-840-6787
no website

Big changes for Teresa Wolf. Formerly a partner at bicoastal Schiowitz/Connor/Ankrum/Wolf, Teresa is now the sole owner of Wolf Talent Group. An actor before Honey Sanders made her an agent, Teresa also worked at Penny Luedtke and Waters Nicolosi.

Teresa says she shares clients and is still good friends with the new west coast version of her former partners now called Connor Ankrum & Associates and Josh Schiowitz who is now a manager.

Her colleagues Frankie Moran and Kym Smith join her repping a list of impressive clients. Among them are Grainger Hines (*The Knick, The Family Fang, Lincoln, Blue Bloods, Castle, NCIS*), Robin de Jesus (*In the Heights, La Cage Aux Folles, Wicked, Law & Order: SVU, Gun Hill Road*), Bobby Steggert (*Boy, Big Fish, Mothers & Sons, Ragtime, Assistance, My Paris*), Marva Hicks (*Motown, Caroline or Change, Thunder Knocking at the Door*), Sheila Tapia (*Side Effects, CQ/CX*), Matthew Stadelmann (*Muhammad Ali's Greatest Fight*), James Biberi (*Drive, Dead Man Down, Analyze That, Find Me Guilty, The Blacklist, Blue Bloods*), Malachi Weir (*Billions, Brooklyn Animal Control*), Charlotte Booker (*Power*) and Anne O'Sullivan (*Red Oaks*). Teresa reviews all pictures and resumes. Though they have called actors from mailings, primarily their clients are referrals from other clients, casting directors or managers. They have a strict policy of not taking anyone on whose work they haven't seen.

Agent: Teresa Wolf
Client List: 168

chapter 18

Glossary

Actors' Equity Membership Requirements: Rules for membership in the union covering work in the theatre state you must have a verifiable Equity Contract in order to join or have been a member in good standing for at least one year in AFTRA or SAG.

Initiation fee is currently $1100, payable prior to election for membership. Basic dues are $59 twice a year. Additionally, there are working dues: 2.25% of gross weekly earnings from employment is deducted from your check just like your income tax. Exact details of qualifications are available at actorsequity.org/membership/duesfees.asp

Actors' Equity Minimum: There are 18 basic contracts ranging from the low end of the Small Production Contract (from $100 to $390 weekly depending on the size of the theatre) to the higher Production Contract covering Broadway houses, Jones Beach, tours, etc. ($1,000 weekly). Highest is the Business Theatre Agreement, for industrial shows produced by large corporations.

Actors' Unions:

SAG-AFTRA (sagaftra.org) is the newly formed union that resulted by the merger of Screen Actors Guild (SAG) and American Federation of Television and Radio Artists (AFTRA). This union covers actors and broadcasters employed in theatrical motion pictures, as well as all filmed and/or digital television product and radio.

Actors' Equity Association (AEA) is the union that covers actors' employment in the theatre. Commonly referred to as Equity.

Atmosphere: another term for Background performers, a.k.a. Extras.

Audition Tape/Reel: A film or digital sample of your work, usually no longer than six minutes, showcasing either one performance or a montage of scenes of an actor's work. Agents and casting directors prefer samples of professional appearances (film or television), but some will look at material produced for audition purposes only. Usually sent on line, but could be on DVD.

Background Performers: a.k.a. Atmosphere and/or Extras.

Boutique Agency: Just as a clothing boutique is a small store specializing in unique one-of-a-kind items, a boutique agency is usually a smaller agency with a select group of special actors.

Breakdown Services: Started in 1971 by Gary Marsh, the Service condenses scripts and lists parts available in films, television and theatre. Expensive and available to agents and managers only.

Clear: The unions require that the agent check with a freelance actor (clearing) before submitting him on a particular project.

Coogan Account: A Coogan account is a special bank account created to set aside a minimum of 15% of a child's total showbiz earnings which is automatically put into the Coogan Account. Proof of a Coogan account must be on record before any auditions. More at ehow.com/how_2179674_child-coogan-account.html.

Freelance: Term used to describe the relationship between an actor and agent or agents who submit the actor for work without an exclusive contract. New York agents frequently will work on this basis. Los Angeles agents rarely consent to this arrangement.

Going Out: Auditions or meetings with directors and/or casting directors. These are usually set up by your agent but have also been set up by very persistent and courageous actors.

Going to Network: Final step in landing a pilot or series. After the audition process has narrowed the list of choices, actors who have already signed option deals are called back for executive approval or not. Sometimes this process can include an extra callback for people even higher up.

HOLA: (hellohola.org) is an Hispanic service and advocacy organization dedicated to expanding the presence of Hispanic artists in entertainment and media through the education and recognition of emerging artists. HOLA works within the industry to insure that the Hispanic community has equal access to jobs. HOLA sponsors awards, a newsletter and maintains a blog.

Industry Referral: If you are looking for an agent, the best possible way to access one is if someone with some credibility in the business will call and make a phone call for you. This could be a casting director, writer, producer or the agent's mother, just so it's someone somehow connected to the business whose opinion the agent respects. If someone says, "just use my name," they are not recommending you.

Letter of Termination: A legal document dissolving the contract between actor and agent. If you are signed to a SAG-AFTRA franchised agent and decide to leave while your current contract is in effect, SAG-AFTRA provides termination template and instructions: sagaftra.org/files/sag/documents/sag-aftra_sample_termination_letter.pdf.

Major Role/Top of Show: A predetermined fee set by producers which, in most cases, is a non-negotiable maximum for guest appearances on television episodes.

Open Call: Refers to auditions or meetings held by casting directors where no agency representation is required. No individual appointments are given. Usually the call is made in an advertisement in one of the trade newspapers, by flyers or in a news story in the popular press. As you can imagine, the number of people who show up is enormous. You will have to wait a long time. Although management's eyes tend to glaze over after a certain number of hours, actors do sometimes get jobs this way. That's how Barkhad Abdirahman got his Oscar nominated part in *Captain Phillips*.

Overexposed: Term used by nervous buyers (producers, networks, casting directors, etc.) indicating an actor has become too recognizable for their tastes. Frequently he just got off another show and everyone remembers him as a particular character and the buyer doesn't want the public thinking of that instead of his project. A wide gap exists between being popularly familiar and overexposed.

Packaging: This practice involves a talent agency approaching a buyer with a writer, a star, usually a star director and possibly a producer already attached to it. A package may include any number of other writers, actors, producers, etc.

Per Diem: Negotiated amount of money for daily expenses on location or on the road per day.

Pictures: The actor's calling card. An 8x10 black and white or color photograph, glossy or matte finish.

Pilot: The first episode of a proposed television series. Produced so that the network can determine whether there will be additional episodes. There are many pilots made every year. Few get picked up. Fewer stay on the air for more than a single season.

Principal: A role larger than an extra or an Under Five.

Ready to Book: Agent term for an actor judged sufficiently trained and mature to handle himself well in an audition both with the material, and with the buyers. Frequently describes an actor whose progress in classes/work has been monitored and guided by the agent or manager.

Resume: The actor's ID. It lists credits, physical description, agent's name and phone contact.

Right: When someone describes an actor as being right for a part, he is speaking about the essence of an actor. We all associate a particular essence with Bradley Cooper and a different essence with Jonah Hill. One would not expect Cooper and Hill to be considered for the same part. Being right also involves experience and credits. The more important the part, the more credits are necessary to justify being seen.

SAG-AFTRA Membership Requirements: The SAG-AFTRA website details how to qualify at sagaftra.org/content/steps-join. You must produce proof of SAG-AFTRA employment or employment under an affiliated performer's union. The one-time initiation fee is currently $3,000. Basic dues are $201.96 annually in addition to work dues calculated at 1.575 percent of covered earnings up to $500,000.

This money is payable in full, in cashier's check or money order, at the time of application. The fees may be lower in some branch areas. If you are not working, you can go on Honorary Withdrawal which only relieves you of the obligation to pay your dues. You are still in the union and prohibited from accepting non-union work. So wait until you are actually being sought for union work as you can no longer do non-union work once you have joined.

SAG-AFTRA Minimum: (aka scale) As of 7-1-15, SAG Scale rates require $859 daily and $3,145 weekly for employment in films and television. Since the merger of SAG-AFTRA, even agents still have to call SAG often to clarify what the pay might be because the less lucrative AFTRA contracts still apply in various contracts, so rates are not as uniform as they once were.

Scale + 10: The union won't allow a union actor to work for less than

SAG-AFTRA minimum for a day's work. If the actor only gets scale and then has to pay his agent 10%, he would not actually be taking home a scale payment so the employer adds 10% to the actor's price to pay the agent.

Scale: aka minimum – legal rate as determined by union contracts.

Sides: The pages of script containing your audition material. Usually not enough information to use as a source to do a good audition. If casting directors won't provide a complete script, go early (or the day before), and sit in the office to read it. SAG rules require producers to allow actors access to the script (if it's written) although sometimes scripts are so secret that even if you are working the job, you only get to see your pages.

Stage Time: Term used to designate the amount of time a performer has had in front of an audience. Most agents and casting executives believe that an actor can only achieve a certain level of confidence by amassing stage time. They're right.

Submissions: Sending an actor's name to a casting director in hopes of getting the actor an audition for a part. Also, an actor submits picture, resume, reel to agents when looking for representation. More and more these days, such submissions are done online.

Talent: Management's synonym for actors.

Test Option Agreement: Before going to network for a pilot/series, actors must routinely sign a contract stating salary for the pilot and series. The contract is for five years with an option for two more years. All options are at the discretion of management. They can drop you at the end of any season and you are bound by the terms of your contract to stay for the initial five years plus their two one-year options.

Top of Show/Major Role: A predetermined fee set by producers which is a non-negotiable maximum for guest appearances on television episodes. Also called Major Role Designation.

The Trades: Showbiz focused newspapers online or in print. *Backstage* continues to be the best source of information about classes, auditions, casting, etc. that are vital for newcomers and particularly those without representation. Available at Samuel French, Larry Edmunds Bookstore, good newsstands, by subscription or at your local library. In Los Angeles this term usually refers to the daily newspapers *Daily Variety*, *The Hollywood Reporter* and *Deadline.com*

Under Five: An AFTRA contract in which the actor has five lines or fewer. Paid at a specific rate less than a principal and more than an extra. Some times referred to as Five and Under.

Visible/Visibility: Currently on view in film, theatre or television. In this business, it's out of sight, out of mind, so visibility is very important.

chapter _19

Indexes

chapter 20

Endnotes

1. Tim Appelo, *The Hollywood Reporter's List of the top 25 Top Drama Schools*, May 4, 2012

2. Jill Gerston, *Acting Is One Thing, Getting Hired Another*, May 25, 1997

3. Ibid.

4. Jennifer Kingson Bloom, *The Early Bird Gets the Audition*, March 23, 1995

5. Ibid.

6. Paul Rosenfield, *The Careerist's Guide to Survival*, April 25, 1982

7. Catherine Shoard, *Meet the Most Powerful Brit in Hollywood: Col Needham, creator of IMDb.,* May 12, 2013

8. Scott Poudfit, *Out from the Shadows*, January 13, 2000

9. Ibid.

10. Alex Needham, *SXSW film: casting directors lift the secrets of their profession*, March 14 2015

11. Ibid.

12. Paul Rosenfield, *The Careerist Guide to Survival,* April 25, 1982

13. Scott Proudfit, *Out from the Shadows*, January 13, 2000

14. Martha Frankel, *Hiding in Plain Sight*, May 1997

15. Stephen Rebello, *Out of the Woods*, November 1994

16. Ibid.

17. Peter Bart, *Mass CAA Defection Spurs Agents to Show Their Clients a Little Love*, April 14, 2015

18. Ibid.

19. Ibid.

20. Beverly Robin Green, *What You Really Need to Know about Managers and Talent Agents, A Practical Guide*, March, 2001

21. Peter Bart, *Mass CAA Defection Spurs Agents to Show Their Clients a Little Love,* April 14, 2015

22. Chris Gardner and Peter Kiefer, *J. Lo: Ex-manager violated,* July 3, 2003

23. Dave McNary, *Vardalos' Ex--manager Dealt Lawsuit Setback,* September 17, 2003

24. Kim Masters, Stephen Galloway, *The Heads of Major Talent Agencies Speak,* June 12, 2015

25. Claudia Eller and Brian Lowry, *Bitter Shandling-Grey Break-up Strikes a Nerve in Hollywood,* January 23, 1998

26. Lynette Rice and Scott Collins, *It's Garry Shandling's Suit,* February 17-23, 1998

27. Cynthia Litttleton, *TV Talk,* September 18, 2000

28. Judd Appatow, Random House, New York, 2015

29. Franklyn Ajaye, Silman-James Press, 2002

30. Charles Champlin, *Pearls of Wisdom from Liz,* March 31, 1996

31. David Robb, *Protecting Kids On Sets: Third In A Series,* October 20, 2014

32. Dawn C. Chmielewski and Amy Kaufman, *Young, Famous and Vulnerable,* November 6, 2010

33. Ibid.

34. Alexandra Lange, *Do Re Me Me Me!,* November 10, 1997